KT-417-385

WRITE FROM THE HEART

The Extraordinary Real Life Story of Glasgow's Favourite Novelist

Margaret Thomson Davis

B&W Publishing

First published 2006
by B&W Publishing Ltd
99 Giles Street, Edinburgh, EH6 6BZ

ISBN 13 9 781845 020927
ISBN 10 1 84502 092 8

Typeset by RefineCatch Ltd, Bungay, Suffolk
Printed and bound by Creative Print and Design Group Ltd

The anonymous poem 'The Other Child' is from
Coming Through The Darkness,
published by Friends Fellowship of Healing.

To my son, Kenneth Baillie Davis, with much love and admiration as always, and to my grandsons, Martin, Colin and Adam.

1

For years I thought my father was Robinson Crusoe. Then it began to dawn on me that I had been mistaken. He was, in fact, Jim Hawkins who had sailed in the good ship *Hispaniola*.

Every night my father told me and my wee brother, Audley, and sometimes a neighbour's daughter, Esther Kirby, as well, stories of his adventures. Not for us the carefully chosen, gentle tales of Noddy or Peter Rabbit or Jemima Puddleduck to lull us into a safe, contented, dream-free sleep. As well as stories like *Robinson Crusoe* and *Treasure Island* my father told us, in a voice husky with drama and feeling, terrible tales of Sweeney Todd the demon barber. And Maria Marten and the murder in the Red Barn. And Burke and Hare the bodysnatchers.

He related all the stories in the first person and acted them out with fiendish glee. At Christmas he was old Scrooge, the ghosts of Christmas past, present and future, and Marley, all with different ghostly, blood-chilling voices. At Christmas he was also Santa Claus and out of the darkness of our bedroom would come his voice accompanied by a tinkling sound.

'Sound of the sleigh bells,' he'd whisper hoarsely. 'Listen to them coming nearer and nearer!'

I knew that he was hiding behind the door clinking teaspoons together but I never had the heart to tell him I knew. He was having such a marvellous time.

Mostly, though, he swept us away with him to his make-believe land. I'll never forget the look of astonishment and fear on his face – emotions that were immediately mirrored in Audley's saucer eyes as well as my own – when he told us that

1

he'd spied the footprints in the sand. We were there, trembling in apprehension beside him every step of the way as he followed the footprints along the deserted beach. It was almost as terrifying as that time on the *Hispaniola* when we crouched down in the apple-barrel and listened to Long John Silver and watched Silver's knife hovering above our heads. There has never been anything quite so dramatic or vivid or exciting in my life as that moment.

I can still see my father's florid face and huge dark eyes and grey hair cut short and sticking straight up like a wire rug from his scalp. And I can hear his deep, rich voice singing 'Fifteen men on a dead man's chest! Yo, ho, ho, and a bottle of rum!'

This is no doubt enough to give any child psychologist nightmares. However, it enlarged, coloured, heightened my emotions, my sensitivity and my imagination. But it terrified my brother. If my mother was in she'd rush to the rescue and snatch him away to tuck him into his bed. Later when we were cuddled up in bed together, Audley would cling to me and plead, 'You tell me a story now, Margaret.' I knew the story he wanted and needed to hear. It was about a wee girl like me and a wee boy like him that *nice* things happened to, and it had a happy and *safe* ending. The nightly reassurance I managed to give my brother was my first practice in story telling.

Later, after I'd told Audley my story and he'd fallen asleep, I'd lie awake in the darkness listening to my mother raging at my father for acting like a maniac and my father bawling back at her that it was she who was mad.

They didn't do that, though, if Esther Kirby was staying overnight with us. Esther was the daughter of a neighbour and an only child. It was a treat for her, apparently, to spend the night with Audley and me.

Indeed, as far as I'm aware, my mother and father never quarrelled in front of anyone except Audley and me. This made for a confusing state of affairs as far as I was concerned. It was as if there were two different worlds. There was the desperately unhappy secret world behind the closed doors of our tenement flat. Then there was the other world that relations, or neighbours, or friends, or any outsider saw. That world, in comparison, was all sweetness and light. In that world, my father's faults and frailties and social gaffes, if mentioned at all, were spoken of in a bright, affectionate, humorous way. Indeed, I've seen my mother have a group of friends that she was entertaining to afternoon tea in absolute stitches of hilarity with her stories of what my father had said or done on different occasions.

He was a big, powerful man but an excruciatingly shy and private kind of person, except with children, of course. Left alone with children he became a child himself and flung himself into their make-believe world with great gusto. In a social adult environment, however, especially with my mother, he suffered agonies.

She was a slap-happy sociable woman of strong and stubborn will. She believed that when my father was behaving in any way differently from her he was just doing it for the hell of it, out of sheer wicked perverseness. She never let him get away with anything.

If she had visitors in the front room and my father insisted on hiding away in the living room or bedroom, she would purposely call out in a sing-song charming voice from the safety of the front room, 'Sa-a-am! Come on through and say hello to the ladies, dear.'

Eventually, like a trapped animal, my father would appear to stand, anguished-eyed, with one hand on the piano top as if for support. After clearing his throat several times he would say stiffly, 'Good evening, ladies. It's very nice to see you. I do hope you will have a pleasant and enjoyable evening.'

The temptation to succumb to a polite round of applause was almost overwhelming and no one relaxed until he had disappeared again. Looking back, however, I can see that I had the fiction writer's heightened awareness – what Theodore Dreiser called the 'self-identification with every fault, frailty or futility'. I knew how my father felt.

Much later, after everyone had gone, there would be a terrible row, with my mother insisting that he had purposely acted like an idiot in order to make everyone, including her, feel awkward and embarrassed.

'You did that out of downright badness,' she'd accuse.

I never believed that, any more than I believed he meant to terrify my brother with his stories. I don't think Audley blamed him either. And of course most writers I have read about have had someone in their childhood like my father, who told them stories in the same vivid and dramatic way.

Take Oliver Goldsmith, for instance. His first teacher was a very eccentric, romantic type called Tom Byrne who was well versed in the fairy superstitions of the country. In school he often didn't feel like teaching a lesson and just told a story instead. Young Goldsmith's imagination appears to have been much excited by this man's stories. The books from which he learned to read were considered most unsuitable and shocked many people of his time. They were the penny dreadfuls of the eighteenth century. Books like *A History of the Irish Rogues and Rapparees; The Lives of Celebrated Pirates; Moll Flanders; Jack, the Bachelor, the notorious smuggler*; and *The Life and Adventures of James Fency, the Irish Robber*.

When Sir Walter Scott was a child his Aunt Janet read him ballads. His grandmother told him of Border affairs. His uncle thrilled him with exciting stories about the campaigns of the American War of Independence. His brother, who was in the navy, kept him spellbound with stories of hairbreadth escapes and blood-curdling adventures.

Robert Louis Stevenson's father had a romantic imagination and kept his son entertained nightly with tales of ships, roadside inns, robbers and old sailors. The child's nanny, Alison Cunningham, or Cummie, had a strong imagination and a great love of rhetoric and dramatic speech.

'It's you that gave me a passion for the drama, Cummie,' Louis told her on the last occasion they met.

'Me, Master Lou?' she replied. 'I never put foot inside a playhouse in my life.'

'Aye, woman,' said Louis. 'But it was the grand, dramatic way ye had of reciting the hymns.'

Young Robert Burns was also told stirring tales on winter nights, tales of witches and ghosties and fairies, by a relative of his mother called Betty Davidson.

D. H. Lawrence's father could barely sign his name and could only painfully read the daily newspaper. His life and his attitudes to life were primitive and almost entirely animal. Yet the artist's temperament that D. H. Lawrence inherited came from him and not from his mother, for all her better education and her nagging sense of superiority.

Lawrence's father was a good dancer. At one time he even ran a dancing class. He told vivid stories to Lawrence about the countryside and animals while out walking with him. This feeling for nature is reflected in much of Lawrence's work.

The list is endless.

This early stimulation of the imagination, this heightening of the sensitivity and the emotions, is the most important influence in a writer's life. You may well be a happier, more secure and contented child without all this stirring of the emotions but you'd have much less chance of becoming a creative writer.

I believe, however, that a human being is like a tree – the core and root are the creativity we all have in common but the branches are different aspects that you either choose or are drawn to. My brother, as he developed, expressed his creativity in music. As I in time would plod away on my own trying to write fiction, he would shut himself in our front room and try to play the piano. He taught himself laboriously, finding each note on the piano and taking a piece of music bar by bar, practising, practising. I still remember Rachmaninov's *Prelude* because I heard it bar by bar repeated so often when my brother was struggling to bring the piece to life on the piano from the piece of sheet music he'd bought with his pocket money. My mother was a beautiful pianist, a very accomplished one, and she was only too eager to teach Audley how to play. But after a couple of lessons in which he found out the names of the notes on the sheet music and how to find them on the piano, he refused to allow my mother to teach him. She adored him. But right from the beginning, he struggled for independence and to be his own person. I admired him so much for that and although, sadly, he is long gone, I admire him still.

I became completely dominated by my mother and somehow was never able to do anything about it, although I resented it deeply, secretly, at least in my moody, awkward teenage years.

Audley, right from when he was a young boy, refused to be a sissy or a mummy's boy. He ignored her pleas not to go to the baths in case he got a chill, not to play cricket or tennis in case he harmed himself in some way – I can't remember all her excuses for trying to coddle him – but he ignored them. He was never rude to her or angry or unloving, but he continued to do his own thing. He went swimming, he played tennis, he played cricket and he taught himself to become a wonderful pianist.

My mother never offered to give me any lessons but she did allow me to have lessons with a friend of Mrs Kirby's, who was a qualified music teacher. Esther Kirby and I would go every week to this lady's house for our lesson. My main memory of that period, apart from the fact that I never showed any signs of having any talent as a pianist, was the fact that en route to this lady's house, there was a bakery that sold delicious rhubarb tarts. I used to spend some of my pocket money, if not all of it, on buying a couple of rhubarb tarts, which I demolished before arriving at the piano teacher's house. As a result, of course, my hands and face were revoltingly sticky, which could not have endeared me – to say the least – to that music teacher. No, my branch of creativity was not music. But while my brother was persevering in trying to play the piano, I was trying to write.

Not that I ever in my wildest flights of fancy as a child or young adult, imagined that I could become a writer. Despite the power of my father's imagination, such an audacious idea was completely beyond him as well. Writers were a different breed from us. They lived in a different world. Indeed it was hard to imagine that such creatures existed in flesh and blood at all. They were so far removed from the tenement flat in the middle of Glasgow in which we lived. For anyone at that time and in such an environment to have writing pretensions was treated with the utmost suspicion. More than that, it aroused in one's friends, neighbours and relations acute embarrassment, shame, discomfort and downright hostility.

A friend of mine, John Maloney, took this strange itch to write. He was a labourer of Irish descent and had no education worth mentioning. He belonged to a large, decent-living family on which nothing or no one had ever brought disgrace.

When John started shutting himself away in a bedroom, not only to write but to address envelopes to himself and have what he'd written posted back to him, the family didn't know what to make of it. They held a family conference. Then one brother who was elected spokesman had a serious talk with John. All to no effect. Eventually the brother burst out in anguish and frustration, 'There's something far wrong with a man who writes letters to himself! If you'd just been a poof the priest could have talked to you or one of us could have battered you out of it. But what the hell can anybody do about a writer?' A writer was not only beyond the pale but beyond comprehension.

When I made what to me was the most earth-shattering, gloriously happy announcement of my life – of my first acceptance by a publisher – it so happened that some relations were visiting. I'll never forget their response after I'd breathlessly informed the family gathering of my success.

My announcement was met with total silence. Until someone said, 'Well, I'm glad wee Tommy's cold didn't go into his chest after all.' Then, in a great tide of relief from embarrassment, the conversation returned to familiar respectable lines.

I felt terribly ashamed. The unspoken belief had been confirmed, that there always had been something odd about me. I felt isolated and that is why, when I eventually met other struggling working-class writers like John, I took them gratefully to my heart. I loved John as a brother and a dear friend, literally to the day he died.

When John received a cheque for the first story he had accepted, his mother became both frightened and distressed, as if he'd perpetrated some sort of fraud or con trick on the publisher. She ordered him to do the decent thing and send the money back. When John insisted he hadn't done anything dishonest she said there must have been a mistake then, so it was still the right thing to do to send it back.

He had a play accepted for television and the day the first review appeared his mother was shocked and said that theirs has always been a respectable family until then; never once had any of their names been in the paper.

My parents gradually came to terms with the problems of me being a writer, although they never really accepted me as a *real* writer – not like authors they admired. My father never lived to see my first book accepted – something about which I've always been sad. But he was proud when he saw my first short story in print. He always shook his head, though, when I spoke of my ambition to be a novelist.

'I can't see how you can ever be a *real* writer when you haven't had a proper grounding in Shakespeare. If only you'd gone to the university like your mammy and I wanted you to.'

It's amazing how many people think that an academic education is essential to being a writer.

There were two reasons that I didn't want to go to university. I didn't tell them to my mother and father. By that time I was very introverted and inarticulate except for my story telling. I had retreated into the world of my imagination. And I had this unexplainable need to write. In order to do this, I felt I had to learn about all different kinds of people, about jobs, about different ways of life. I just knew that instinctively.

The other reason was that when I was at school, my brother somehow could sit his examinations and get wonderful marks. I remember my mother always boasting about this. He seemed to need to do very little study, if any at all. I, in trying to keep up with him and please my parents – especially my mother – was studying every night and even so, I had a terrible struggle to get decent marks in my examinations. Right enough, when I think of it, I got eight O levels before I left school so I must have passed every exam I sat, but I do remember it as a most stressful business and a terrible struggle. I suppose I just wanted to be free of it all. Maybe if I'd been able to explain this to my parents, they might have understood. I wasn't able to, however, and they were very disappointed in me when I dug my heels in and refused to go to university.

To be honest, I wouldn't even have stayed on at school to sit my O levels if I'd had my way but I was defeated by my mother in this. I had actually fixed up with a job in Grant's bookshop in town. In celebration of what I thought was my first step into adulthood and the world of books, I slept with my head covered in rag curlers and on the morning of the big day I combed my hair into a fashionably smooth 'page-boy'. (I'd always hated my curly Shirley Temple-type hair.)

But when my mother heard that I was off to start work in Grant's bookshop instead of going to school (I didn't have the nerve to tell her until the last moment), and when she saw my smooth hairstyle, she grabbed a brush and me, and battered and tugged the brush unmercifully over my head. She didn't stop until I was the most ghastly frizzy mess you've ever seen. My hair was literally standing on end all over. Then, despite my wails and brokenhearted sobbing and my red swollen face, she marched me into the centre of the city to Grant's bookshop. There she demanded to see the manager and told him that I was not starting after all because I had to stay on at school and then go to university for a decent education.

Years later, after my books were published, my mother became aggressively loyal and insisted to everyone that I was a writer of tremendous talent, well thought of in the highest circles.

But in private she sighed and shook her head and cried out to me in despair, 'Why can't you write *nice* books like Annie S. Swan?'

2

D. H. Lawrence showed an advance copy of his first book *The White Peacock* to his mother and later he said, 'She looked at the outside and then at the title page and then at me with darkening eyes. And though she loved me so much, I think she doubted whether it could be much of a book, since no one more important had written it . . . It was put aside, and I never wanted to see it again. She never saw it again . . .'

His father's reaction was typical and crushing.

'And what dun they gi'e thee for that, lad?'

'Fifty pounds, Father.'

'Fifty pounds!' He was dumbfounded and looked at his son with shrewd eyes, as if he was a swindler. 'Fifty pounds! An' tha's niver done a day's hard work in thy life!'

This is the problem a tyro writer has to grapple with. No one he knows regards writing as work.

Often my mother burst out in harassment when she found me sitting in some corner with a notebook and pencil on my knee, 'There's a lot more important things you could be doing than sitting there scribbling. Give that floor a good scrub, for instance.'

At night it infuriated my father the way I kept the light on till all hours. He was always reminding me that electricity cost money and to see me burning money away anyone would think I was determined that he should end his days in the poorhouse.

My father had the loan of a typewriter from the union when he was branch secretary and as soon as he found out I was using it he was so outraged he locked it away in the lobby cupboard. At the time I was young and selfishly obsessed with, as Maupassant said, 'getting black on white', and I made no attempt to understand my father. I just seethed with resentment and hatred.

I realise now that my poor father was much tormented and hard put to it to guard his belongings from my mother. (She would give things away at the drop of a hat. She once gave away to an old beggar woman a ring that had been given to me by my first boyfriend and was of great sentimental value.) Having to contend with me as well was more than his flesh and blood could stand.

Every effort to secure a private area of his life where he could be himself was scattered before the wind of my mother's cheerful carelessness.

His good hide-leather chair that he'd saved for for years and regarded, next to his books, as his most precious possession was violated by teacup rings on the arms and holes where needles and pins had been stuck in. Its velvet cushion was lumped out of shape with newspapers, magazines, combs, hairbrushes, biscuit crumbs, stockings and knickers being stuffed underneath.

He could never find his socks or his cufflinks although he'd put them carefully away in his drawer. The towel he insisted on having for his own was invariably found lying wet where my mother had abandoned it. I've seen him go grey in the face and saucer-eyed with rage over my mother using his towel.

'You're mad,' she used to say. 'Away ye go and don't annoy me!'

His need to hang on to a bit of himself was as strong and as wild as my obsession with writing. I'm so sorry I was unable to cope with this in my teens. If I had been, I might have managed to avoid some bitter explosions between us. Like the time I decided to get up an hour or so earlier than I normally needed to, in order to get some writing done before leaving for work. I made the thoughtless error of taking my father's alarm clock (the only clock in the house), with the intention of resetting it and returning it to him in the morning.

Now, it was my father's pride that he had never been late for his work in his life and never taken a day off except when he had double pneumonia. For this obsessive conscientiousness he depended on the alarm clock. No one had ever been allowed to touch it.

He wound it every night with loving care and, believe it or not, in winter he used to wrap a woollen scarf round it because the cold seemed to affect its workings. It affected our workings as well, as a matter of fact. That house was cold. If central heating had been invented we certainly had never heard of it and couldn't have afforded it if we had.

Anyway, my father got himself into a state of extreme agitation when he discovered his clock was not in its accustomed place. My explanations and assurances were to no avail. He loudly wanted his clock back. In a burst of frustration at the unfairness of life I threw the clock at him from the other end of the room. I can still see the horror on his face as he watched it bounce across the floor; the way his skin went a sickly grey and showed the stubble on his cheeks and chin, the way his dark eyes became anguished. I'm sure he wouldn't have felt nearly so upset if I'd bounced my mother across that floor.

Tenderly he picked the clock up. He gazed at it, put his ear to it like an anxious doctor at a patient's chest. Then he wound it with meticulous care before wrapping it in a warm scarf and placing it beside his bed. All this time my mother was telling him he'd drive anyone to throw things at him, the way he behaved, and that there were places for people like him in Hawkhead (the asylum) and that he just tormented us all out of sheer badness. But later she came marching into my room and said, 'That was a terrible thing to do to your daddy. God was watching you, you know, and He doesn't forget.'

My father didn't say anything until next morning when he kissed me cheerio before going to his work.

'I'm sorry, hen,' he said.

He was always the first one to apologise, indeed the only one if the altercation was between him and my mother. At least, my mother never apologised verbally in my hearing or to my knowledge.

I often wish I could have some of her supreme confidence in herself and in what she believed.

I remember early in my own marriage I had a quarrel with my husband and I made the mistake of pouring out my grievances to my mother. Her loyalty to me knew no bounds and she assured me that she would soon sort out that 'devil' and that after she was finished telling him a thing or two the 'wicked creature' wouldn't dare behave like that to me again.

Realising my mistake, I tried to calm the storm of indignation I'd raised.

'But, Mummy, there's two sides to every quarrel, you know.'

'I know,' she said. 'You're right and he's wrong!'

It was the same principle she held to in her own marriage which, it seemed to me, was a continuous battleground. The only thing I can recall my mother and father ever agreeing on was that I should go to university.

My writing was never taken seriously enough for them to make an issue of it. It wasn't brought into any discussion of my future. If I was asked what I most wanted to do and I honestly said I wanted to write it was usually suffered with an indulgent 'Aye, we know, hen, but what do you want to *work* at?'

I never mentioned the embarrassing subject of writing to anyone else, although I'd always told stories. First of all to my wee brother in bed every night. Then during the day at school I told stories in the playground – serial stories that ended with a cliffhanger at the sound of the bell and continued at the next playtime. I knew instinctively to end with that cliffhanger just before the bell so that I could make sure they all came back to me. It was my way of getting attention. I wasn't really committing anything of myself as I'm doing in this book or as I have done in my novels. I didn't know enough, if anything, about myself then. I've heard famous comedians say that they started in school by telling funny stories and making other children laugh in whatever way they could. They did this to avoid being bullied and to be liked instead. Acting the clown was a kind of survival kit for them. For me it was telling exciting suspense and adventure stories in serial form.

After school, especially during the dark winter evenings, I dictated ghost stories and tales of horror to my girlfriend, who was taking a secretarial course and needed practice with her shorthand. As a result I was so frightened by my imaginings that I used to hare across the road from her place to my own as if all the fiends of hell were after me. We lived in the top flat then and I took the stairs three at a time and nearly battered the door down in my anxiety to get into safety.

At the time of the Empire Exhibition an uncle and aunt came from some country area – I can't remember where – and took Audley and me to the exhibition with them for a treat. Despite all my story telling – or maybe because of it – I was a timid child and when it came to sampling the thrills of the amusement park I hung back. I was a right spoilsport and refused to set foot on even the slowest and most harmless-looking roundabout. My wee brother had a lot more courage and eventually, thoroughly sick of me and my 'stupid carry-on', my aunt and uncle left me to my own devices and concentrated on sharing all the scream-raising amusements with Audley.

Next day at school my classmates were eager for news of my adventures. I didn't let them down. Never, I'm sure, had they heard of such a colourful and dangerous amusement park or anyone who showed more courage in sampling its dangers than me.

I suppose that was just an extension of my stories to Audley and Esther. Sometimes, looking back, it seems that I quite often had stories thrust upon me, like the Christmas when Audley asked Santa for a Meccano set. Meccano sets were expensive. At least, they were to a family like ours. Recently a friend of mine was telling me how poor her family had been.

'Margaret,' she said in hushed tones, 'we even had frayed dinner napkins!'

I had to smile. I never even knew dinner napkins existed when I was young.

As I've already mentioned, my mother adored my wee brother, and no wonder. He was such a lovable child with his chubby cheeks, large round eyes and breathless enthusiasms. There was never any hiding how Audley felt. He also had long thick lashes and a mop of curly hair which he said he hated because it was 'sissy'. He was an excitable and active child and he had the courage to fight against his many fears. This led him into lots of scrapes and adventures. But there were times when he could quietly become engrossed with plasticine. The stuff seemed to come to life in his hands and my mother took great pride in showing off to friends models he made.

But this Christmas he asked not for plasticine but for a Meccano set. I could see, even then, how my mother could not deny him it and I'm glad she didn't. He was always a bit delicate, despite his baby plumpness. Later in his teens he became gaunt and enormous-eyed from the pain he suffered with rheumatic fever. The heart condition it left him with killed him when he was still a young man.

The rheumatic fever was the result, I'm sure, of the damp bedroom he slept in. The wallpaper used to puff darkly off the walls and every night my mother used to try to dry his blankets and mattress in front of the living room fire. I well remember the steam rising from them.

So when Audley asked Santa for the Meccano set, my mother was determined that by hook or by crook she was going to get him one. But her housekeeping had always been run on the 'rob Peter to pay Paul' method and it must have taken quite a bit of financial juggling, desperate con tricks, and sheer nerve to get the price of one out of her pittance of housekeeping money. She managed it. Unfortunately it meant she couldn't buy one other thing that Christmas – not even an orange for a stocking and certainly not a present for me.

I remember how before Christmas she drew me aside and asked, 'Would you like half a Meccano set for Christmas, Margaret?'

Knowing how Audley longed for one and sensing that it would please my mother if I said yes, I said yes . . .

I loved my brother and accepted without any conscious thought and – as far as I can honestly remember – without any jealousy, that my mother loved him better than me. I never believed, in fact, that she loved me at all but I just accepted this as the normal order of things. I tried to please her, though, on the off-chance that it might help. And it did please her when I said I wanted half a Meccano set for Christmas.

However, at the back of my mind, I still believed that Santa would bring me a doll as well. But Christmas morning came and there on the rug in front of the living room fire (usually a black smoky fire, I remember – 'banked up with dross') sat one solitary box of Meccano.

Instinctively I knew that it was vitally important for me and my likeability rating to hide my true feelings. This I managed to do.

Then later that day when a neighbour asked me what I'd got for Christmas I told her in detailed and dramatic terms of how I had received a chocolate handbag and when I opened it there was a chocolate purse and when I opened that, inside I found lots and lots of chocolate money.

I mention the incident of the 'Meccano Christmas' not only because of the story I told about it but because it was a small yet important step in the development of the intuition and the need to communicate that are necessary for a novelist.

3

What did I need to communicate? I didn't know – not then. If anything, I think instinctively I was trying not to communicate my feelings, in case I made the situation worse. I was frightened even to think about them myself. There were so many things I didn't understand, indeed cannot understand even yet, although as a novelist I never give up trying. Why, for instance, did my kindly good-living Christian mother sometimes reveal what I can only think must have been disgust and hatred of me? Why, for instance, did she neglect to bathe me when I was a small child? I remember when she was forced to strip me and put me in a bath to avoid the shame of this neglect being found out at a school medical examination. I remember the sight of my body, grey with ingrained dirt. I remember her averted eyes as she roughly scrubbed my skin.

I suppose we are all victims of victims. Who knows what trauma my mother suffered when she was a child. She certainly had some sort of Victorian hang-up about sex. The word never passed her lips. I, of course, grew up in complete ignorance about my body and anything to do with sex. I remember a girlfriend asking me to come with her and some other girls and boys from school to the swimming baths. She said she'd loan me her sister's swimming costume. I dashed upstairs to tell my mother that I was off to the swimming baths with Mary and Daisy and Johnny and Peter. That's as far as I got. My mother was horrified. 'What? Going to the swimming baths with boys? You wicked girl, you certainly will not!' Her eyes averting from me, the twist of her mouth as she turned her face away has stayed with me all down through the years.

I couldn't for the life of me understand what was wicked about swimming baths and boys. I was mystified. I didn't know what to say to my friends, what excuse to make.

It was strange but my mother used to give the impression of being very romantic and quite a matchmaker among her friends. She certainly did not give the impression to outsiders that she was in any way repressed or prudish. She was actually a lovely, kindly, cheery person much beloved by all her friends and rightly so, because she was a good friend.

She used to speak of her happy childhood as the only surviving girl in a big extrovert family of boys. The whole family had at one point saved up to buy my mother a piano and pay for her to have music lessons. To the outside world, to all outward appearances, she was happy still. We were a normal happy family.

It's strange how I felt part of it, because I knew nothing else – that was my world, yet at the same time not part of it. Let me try to illustrate the sort of thing that made me feel this isolation. This is only a small trivial kind of incident, I suppose, but they all mount up to give a certain feeling or impression.

It was a Sunday and that was the day that the ice cream vans came around. Now we hadn't a lot of money to spend on luxuries like ice cream, so this particular day, it was a special event, a special treat. We were going to have ice cream and I was given a jug and money and told to go and get the jug filled at the van. This was a serious responsibility for me at the time. It was desperately important that I proved my worth and made a success of the task. I got the ice cream and came rushing back upstairs, eager to please everybody. For some reason, both my mother and father were standing in the doorway watching for me, waiting for me. Whether it was to encourage me or just because they were eager to get stuck into the ice cream, I don't know. In my eagerness to be quick and complete my important task, I must have been running too quickly because I fell on the stairs, tumbled down, the jug smashed, and the precious ice cream splashed out. The point of this is, my father looked furious and my mother turned away. Both of them seemed disgusted but my mother said to my father as she turned back into the house, 'She didn't mean to do it.' Well, that was all right, I suppose, but the point is she was speaking to him and they had both turned away from me and left me shut out.

Now, had that incident happened many years later when I had a young child – if my wee boy Kenneth had fallen among broken glass as I did – I would have rushed downstairs to him and caught him up and said things like, 'Are you all right, son? You're not cut, are you? Now don't worry, it's all right as long as you're all right. The ice cream doesn't matter as long as you're all right.' And I would have hugged him and kissed him and comforted him. Wouldn't that be a more natural thing to do? I suppose I was even left to clean it all up but I can't honestly remember. What I do remember is that turning away, that shutting me out.

Of course it was a different time, a different age. Maybe all children were treated differently then. There used to be that saying, 'Children should be seen and not heard.' Maybe that gives a clue to the difference. There seemed to be a lack of understanding of children as individuals in their own right and with genuine feelings of their own.

I remember Audley was very attached to a soft toy in the shape of a black Scottie dog. Maybe it became too shabby or dirty. I don't know. Anyway, one day my mother threw it out. Later, when Audley found out, he rescued it from the outside midden. My mother found him cuddling the dog in bed that night. It was covered in ash and other debris from the midden. Next day she washed it and all its stuffing sank in one matted lump to its tail end. Nevertheless, Audley still insisted on clinging to it.

Mind you, when I think of it, if Audley had fallen with that jug of ice cream, I cannot imagine her turning away from him as she did with me. I believe she would have acted in that situation with Audley as I've already explained I would have done with my wee boy. I think the difference can only be explained by her attitude towards me. The explanation for that may be quite simply that I wasn't a lovable or even a likeable child.

Perhaps that is why now, when I'm a successful novelist, I'm so keenly appreciative of the fans who write to me or come up to me to shake my hand and speak to me after I've given a talk in some bookshop or library or wherever. They tell me how they've enjoyed my books and how they are so glad of the opportunity to meet me and thank me for all the many hours of pleasure I've given them.

So often people use these same words and each time I hear them, it's like the first time. I feel so lucky and so happy. I felt even more than that recently when a woman came up to me and, with tears in her eyes, gave me a hug and told me that she had been the victim of a serious physical attack and afterwards had lost confidence in herself. She had in fact suffered a nervous breakdown. A woman psychologist (or psychiatrist, I can't remember) advised her to read Margaret Thomson Davis's books. First of all, she said they would take her completely out of her own world and into the world of the author. She would experience how the characters in the book suffered but came through their suffering and were strengthened and expressed hope for the future. The woman thanked me and hugged me again. I was speechless. I was so moved. For the first time I felt I had really done something worthwhile with my writing. To me, my readers are like my friends. The wonderful thing is, I seem to have so many of them, not just in Glasgow but all over the country and indeed in quite a few countries overseas.

Back in those childhood days, though, I didn't realise that so many friends and so much good luck awaited me in the future.

I often tell beginner writers now that an unhappy childhood is a great asset to a novelist. But, I must admit, it didn't seem to be much of an asset at the time.

4

I come back to the work aspect because it links in with lack of confidence, especially beginner writers' lack of confidence, their lack of belief that they could become an author. One of the biggest stumbling blocks, if not the main hurdle to overcome, is this sense of disbelief, of unreality, in yourself and others. Once you get over that, then it's a matter of perseverance and learning to develop the characteristics and techniques that are needed to become a published writer.

Don't expect people's attitudes to change as soon as you get your first story published, however. When relations and friends hear that some editor or publisher has actually parted with good money for one of your stories the chances are they'll regard it as being the result of luck, not work.

In this context, someone once said to Mark Twain that he was lucky and he replied, 'Yes and the harder I work, the luckier I get!'

There's another attitude widely held and that is that anyone could write a marvellous book *if they had the time*. You've no idea how often a writer is told this. A novelist friend of mine had the plasterer in her house doing a job recently and he made the usual remark, 'I could write a marvellous book . . .' My friend waited for the infuriating bit and it came – 'if I had the time!'

That does get annoying and, as it happened, my friend felt a bit tetchy, so she said, 'Well, even if I was given all the time in the world, I'd never be able to plaster a wall.'

The plasterer answered, 'No, I don't believe you could because you need a flair for it.'

I used to feel very bitter at one stage about not being able to get published. I looked at all the sugar-plum-fairy-tale-happy-ever-after stories about twinkly-eyed heroes and blonde blue-eyed heroines in women's magazines and I wept with frustration at how far removed from real life they were. And here was I only too well aware of the honest horrors of real life and nobody wanted to know. It was terribly galling. Especially when I needed the money. I burned with hatred at the unfairness and stupidity of editors and publishers. But not for long.

There comes a time when you've got to make a choice. Either you remain a self-pitying failure with a closed mind and a chip on your shoulder. Or you take a deep breath, gird your loins, and try to learn where you're going wrong in the presentation of what you honestly want to say. Then determine to continue serving your apprenticeship by practice, practice, practice until you can say it successfully as well as honestly and so reach your public.

Then what does it take? It takes imagination and it helps, as I've already suggested, if a writer's imagination was fired by being told stories in a highly stimulating and dramatic way in the formative years. Yes, a writer must have imagination, a very special kind of imagination and not only in dramatic intensity. It is tied up with another important part of a writer's equipment – an insatiable curiosity about people and what makes them tick. Imagination, the ability to find out how others live and how they would want to live are, I believe, the basis of literature.

Henry James spoke of the writer's 'power to guess the unseen from the seen, to trace the implications of things, to judge the whole piece by the pattern, the condition of feeling life in general so completely that you are well on your way to knowing any particular corner of it'.

I believe in intuition as well. My dictionary defines intuition as being the power of seeing the truth directly without reasoning. Intuition can be sharpened and developed with practice. Practice – that is another essential. A writer needs practice in observation, practice in writing and practice in developing intuition.

A writer can appear slow-witted and absent-minded yet can at the same time have the speed of light in picking up, seizing on any tiny give-away sign or word or look or gesture. It's a selectivity of *significant* things. It's an alertness, an immediate and instinctive switching on to something that is in his line of business, the business of people and what makes them tick. It's something that comes with practise.

Katherine Mansfield said, 'Here are the inevitables – the realisation that Art is absolutely self-development. The knowledge that genius is dormant in every soul – that that very individuality which is at the root of our being is what matters so poignantly.'

Everyone who has ever wanted to write and had any secret dreams of becoming a writer should write down those words of Katherine Mansfield's, learn them off by heart, look at them and repeat them every day at least half a dozen times. *And believe them implicitly.*

5

No, you don't need an academic qualification to become a creative writer. You don't need a professorship, a PhD or an MA. You don't even need any A or O levels. These things, *while highly commendable and excellent in themselves* (many writers have academic qualifications, many do not), are irrelevant and immaterial as far as *creativity* is concerned.

It helps, as John Braine believed, to have a lively and interesting mind as opposed to a dull one and most writers have at some time in their lives enjoyed reading a lot of books. But once you start writing you haven't much time for reading, unless it's research material that you need to read to help you with what you want to write. Somerset Maugham said, 'I am not a scholar, a student or a critic, I am a professional writer and now I read only when it is useful to me, professionally.'

Some people think it needs a particular kind of cleverness to write a historical novel and they have said to me, 'I could never write a historical novel. I could never have learned as much as you did, for instance, to write your eighteenth-century books. I could never hold all that information in my mind.'

Nor could I. I didn't need to. I know where to find the information when I want it. But more about that when I deal with research in another chapter.

The point I want to make just now is that the job of the academic, especially the lecturer in an English department of a university, and that of a creative writer are completely different.

So many people believe that because a person works at a university, lecturing in English, it naturally follows that they will be able to *produce* what they talk about. Nothing is further from the truth. I stress this because for years I suffered from the delusion that academic knowledge about literature was the key to being able to write it. I regarded the academic's knowledge of literature and ability to be articulate about it with such awe and admiration that I was painfully inhibited by it, or rather by my lack of knowledge and lack of ability to be articulate in comparison.

The truth was brought home to me slowly – incredibly by meeting innumerable and brilliant academics who wanted to write, who *longed* to write, but simply couldn't do it. By 'write' I mean create original fiction. The vast majority of them can put on paper theories or theses or works of criticism about creative writers but cannot become one themselves.

Long after I was a published writer, making a decent income from my writing, and my books were getting excellent reviews, I was still labouring under the delusion that, if I went to extramural classes at the university and listened to the tutors there, I would learn how to be a better writer. They, with their superior knowledge of literature, would be able to teach me. At first I found the classes interesting, then I became restless, then bored, then absolutely infuriated and near to exploding with impatience at the way the lecturer and the students endlessly analysed novels. Chapter by chapter, paragraph by paragraph, sentence by sentence, everything was picked over and turned inside out and back to front in their efforts to find not one but a hundred and one different meanings. Each and every character was psychoanalysed. Countless guesses were made regarding what the characters would have done in other circumstances quite different from those of the story in which they belonged.

Eventually I couldn't help thinking, 'What the hell am I doing here? Nobody, *especially* the tutor, knows a damned thing about writing. Not *how to do it!*'

I found myself becoming more interested in the tutor and the students as people. I sat watching them, their individual mannerisms and characteristics and wondered what they were really like inside and what kind of lives they led. I listened to what they said and wondered *why* they said it. I suppose I was listening with a writer's ear and observing with a writer's eye but I didn't mean it to be obvious. The fact that it must have become uncomfortably so was brought home to me when a male student drew me aside one evening as we were leaving.

'It might look as if there's something going on between me and Mrs Brown,' he said, 'but I can assure you our friendship is absolutely innocent!'

There was material for at least two dozen novels in that room and each person there was a character ready for the picking. In fact, if you take any person from real life and push them to their limits, you have a character for a novel.

The most fascinating thing I learned by attending these classes, however, was the approach the tutors had to writing. I had and still have a great admiration for academics but I am now convinced that if you want to learn how to write creative fiction it is not to the academic you should turn for illumination. The only person who can help the beginner (apart from himself or herself) is a published creative writer.

Writers talking about writing are so practical in comparison.

I've been to many writers' schools and conferences and heard innumerable writers lecture and they really got down to brass tacks, never mind the theorising. The exception to this has been those writers who have been academics as well.

I have been in an audience of 300 writers, a mixture of successful professionals and others at different stages of their apprenticeship, and the lecturer turned out to be on sabbatical from some university. I have known a lecturer like this to reveal intellectual snobbishness and be subtly patronising to the audience. Not that it mattered, because it made him interesting to observe as a person and I could just imagine 300 minds beavering away as they secretly analysed him and wondered how they could use him in a story. But as his very literary thesis wound on its complicated way, the audience began to get restless. Some dozed off.

Other academics and writers kept you alert and interested by their sheer brilliance at composing and delivering a good lecture. It impressed and even entertained the audience. It gave them angles on how to be a successful speaker. It was seldom, however, much help to a struggling writer who wanted to know how to *write* successfully.

An academic who is also a writer is only of practical help when the writer part of him, the creative part, is strongest.

Creativity is upset by analysis. If you attempt to write a story with parts of your mind pulling and worrying about whether you're doing it to the 'proper rules' or if you're haunted by learned critics breathing over your shoulder, the chances are your mind will block. You won't be able to write anything at all. At best it will spoil the sweep and faith in your story that is essential if you're going to write it. It will murder your courage in continuing and your pleasure in going on. Few writers are able to write against these handicaps.

As Malcolm Cowley said in one of the Hopwood Lectures:

> The sort of training that is best for a future critic or teacher –
> the sort given in our best universities – is often dangerous to
> an apprentice writer. If he spends too much time on the close
> analysis of texts, the critical side of him ceases to be a listener,
> making its critical comments in an undertone; the voice of the
> critic becomes louder, firmer, more admonitory, and perhaps
> the other voice, that of instinct or emotion, may be frightened
> back into the depths of the mind.

Writing, I repeat, is a different ball game altogether.

6

Feelings, good or bad, are definitely important and the stronger the better. In fact, better still, a writer should write from something that obsesses him or her. Apart from anything else, this gives the drive, the desperate energy needed to complete book after book.

Once a beginner writer was chatting to me and told me his girlfriend's ex was stalking her and pestering her with threatening letters, and so on. The beginner writer eventually burst out emotionally, 'I could kill him!'

'Well,' I replied, 'do it, but in a novel. That way the emotion will be true and believable and that's the important thing in any successful novel. The situation, the characters, their jobs, and so on, can all be different but the emotion must be there.'

There's also got to be an obsession with the actual writing, with the putting of words down on paper. Lots of writers I know, including myself, even have an affection for the paper and all the accoutrements of writing. I really enjoy looking in a stationer's window or wandering about inside the shop. The sight of all that virgin paper, all those lovely notebooks and pens and pencils fills me with pleasure and satisfaction, even happiness. This is something else one's non-writer friends don't understand. I knew exactly how my friend John Maloney felt when he said to me, 'I wish to God my family and friends would stop giving me presents of socks and soap and bloody aftershave at Christmas, Margaret. If only they'd give me something useful, something I'd really appreciate – like a ream of typing paper!'

I knew at the beginning that I had the obsession with putting words down on paper. I was not aware at the time, however, of the deeper obsessive feelings I suffered from and still suffer from.

I started to write little descriptions of things that caught my attention; a tree, a sunset, the moon, clouds. Clever-sounding phrases that occurred to me were recorded in my notebook. Brief pen-sketches of people that I met or noticed in the street were conscientiously included. I also kept a diary.

As far as I can remember I have never used anything from these notebooks or diaries. I don't regret them, though. I was developing a love of words. I was practising writing words down. But, most important of all, I was developing observation, intuition and selectivity. These things at that far-off time were weak and undernourished but they were there. I was using my eyes. I was interested in people and things around me. Something, I didn't know what, made me pick out certain people and certain things. The observation of *significant* things is vitally important. It ties up with *selectivity*.

Now, I believe that there is creativity in everyone and it can be channelled into all sorts of pursuits like sewing and knitting and cooking and carpentry and sculpture and painting and writing and so on. Whatever creative thing you feel you want to do, if you work hard enough at it and learn enough about it, you'll do it and do it successfully.

So much, though, in this writing business is intuitive. I know I'm on difficult ground here. Trying to explain what this instinct is and how to develop and sharpen it is like trying to grasp shadows or mountain mist and pin them under a microscope. I think the best way to illustrate what I mean is to keep revealing wisps of my own experience.

My earliest instinctual memory, for instance, is a vague feeling of being in a cot. Through the darkness of time I caught glimpses of wooden cot bars. I concentrated my attention on this experience, this feeling of being in a cot. Soon I became aware of being near an old-fashioned black grate with a gas mantle above it to its right side. I didn't have a clear picture of this in my mind's eye. Yet the more I concentrated – not so much my mind but my *senses* on the scene – I *knew* that the cot was in a small room in front of a fireplace and close at the side of a high set-in-the-wall bed. On that bed lay the humped figure of my mother. I had not so much sight – everything was dark and shadowy and incomplete – but the *impression* of these things.

I didn't feel any pain or remember any sound but I knew I was crying. Then I had the sensation of a man bending over the cot, lifting me out and dressing me in a tiny velvet dress. It was dark red in colour. My memory wasn't in colour. Everything was still in shadow. I just felt that it was dark red in the same way that I knew the man was my father.

Now comes what to me is the most interesting and significant bit. I felt, coming from the bed in which my mother lay, a wave of absolute hatred. More than hatred. It was repulsion. It was that emotion emanating from my mother that returned to me most clearly and vividly remained with me ever since.

That feeling that my mother hated and rejected me affected my whole life more than I can say. And it's only recently – sadly, long after my mother's death – that two things occurred to me. One, my mother might have been pregnant with my wee brother at the time and feeling unwell and not able to get up and attend to me herself. And, two, if I was screaming and screaming and she felt ill and unable to cope and just longed for a bit of peace and quiet, wasn't it natural that the poor soul would – even if just for that night or that moment – hate me? She could have loved me again the next minute or the next day but I just didn't remember that. Although, to be honest, I still can't think of any examples of love for me.

I suppose that early scene has affected not only my life but also my books but there's a lot more to my novels than that.

There is, I hope, first and foremost what one tutor wrote in red ink on an essay I had attempted on the subject he'd given, which was the Poor Law of 1834. He wrote alongside my fail mark, 'But what a cracking good tale you've made of it.'

I doubt if I will ever write a good essay but I hope I'll always be able to tell a good story that will interest and entertain as well as help people to understand each other better.

To do this, of course, you've got to work at trying to understand yourself.

You see, writing isn't finding or deciding on a subject to write about. Writing is *being*.

Pearl S. Buck said, 'Writing novels absorbs the entire life and being. If the sacrifice of life and being is not joyfully made, then it should not be made at all.'

7

Dylan Thomas said he wrote poems as stepping stones out of his own darkness. I think this indicates not only the quest for understanding that I have been talking about but a cathartic element in a man's or woman's writing. It is Maugham's 'disembarrassment of the soul'. Although, of course, a writer may not be conscious of this while working on a novel. Yet while working on a novel, a writer must be supremely and courageously himself or herself.

Mostly I'm a background person. I leave others to enjoy the limelight and do the talking. That way I'm free to listen and watch, to observe people. But I'm tuning in to them as much if not more with my 'emotional antennae' than with my ears and eyes. From that first intuitive experience as a baby these antennae have developed, with much concentration over the years. They have flourished in rich soil.

As I mentioned earlier, my brother was a delicate lad and my mother, quite understandably, lavished much more time, attention and love on him than she did on me. I didn't understand at the time. She was always leaving my father and she'd take Audley with her but leave me. As a result, when I set off for school each morning, I could never be sure if she and my brother would be there when I returned or what was going to happen to me. I'm talking about a five-year-old and primary school onwards, although I have shadowy nightmare memories of being left at an even earlier age. But even to a child of primary-school age this is, to say the least, an insecure lifestyle. Every morning before I set off for school I used to kiss my mother, then gaze up at her, desperately trying to tune into her, to sense if she was going to leave me.

Every single day after I went out and shut the door, I had to force myself to walk away from it. I had this compulsion to knock and bring her back to me so that I could kiss her once again.

She used to get so irritated with me I'm sure she could have cheerfully strangled me. I felt the irritation straining out even though she struggled valiantly to control it. Only once did she ever strike me and I haven't the slightest recollection of the actual blow. All I remember is that one day she called me over to her knee and apologised for 'raising her hand'.

All day and every day at school what the teacher said or did, what the other children said or did, only skimmed vaguely over the surface of my attention. It reminds me of what Harold Robbins once said when talking about how he felt while writing a novel: 'I'm right here, and yet I'm not right here. I'm doing everyday things I have to do and yet my head is somewhere else. And I never really come together.'

I just existed, hung in suspense from the moment I left the house until I returned there again. Tension would mount as I approached the road, then the building, and by the time I entered the close and reached the doorstep I was on the point of secret collapse. I knocked at the door and waited, my whole being centred on listening for my mother's jaunty stride along the lobby, willing it to come.

If I peered through the letterbox and saw newspapers spread over the linoleum and smelled disinfectant, I knew she had gone.

Normally my mother had a cheerful disregard for housework. But when she left my father she always did so in a burst of cleaning and scrubbing as if literally washing her hands of him forever.

I would stand for a while on the doormat before going to sit on the stone steps of the close. I wasn't trying to remember what shift my father was on and when he'd be home. I wasn't wondering if my mother would be away for a day or a week or a month. She'd gone and I was in a state of shock.

Looking back, this kind of experience has been invaluable to me because it wonderfully concentrated my sensitivities. For one thing I know how a child can feel. I know that ideas of time, the past, the future, mean nothing. There is no future.

Eventually neighbours would see me and take me in. They were kind but I sensed what a nuisance I was hanging about, albeit quietly, while they were busy making their tea. As soon as I saw from the window my father coming along the street, I would make my way slowly downstairs. My father was a man of uncertain temper and the discovery of the loss of my mother was always a terrible thing to behold. What's more, to be lumbered yet again with me was an extra punishment and a very difficult situation indeed because, for one thing, when he was on night shift or back shift, it meant he would have to find someone to look after me. But first I'd have to go down with him to Springburn to the pub and wait outside for what seemed an eternity while he drowned his sorrows.

The awful thing as far as I was concerned was that I was not looked after. I was abused. I didn't know at the time what was happening, only that I was terrified. And what does a five-year-old know about what's normal and what's not in life, what should happen and what should not? No one talked about child abuse in those days. Did anyone know that it existed, I wonder?

It's only recently that I've been able to talk about it myself and I'm now a pensioner and a grandmother. I realise now that in one way it affected and ruined my whole life and I'll never get over it. In another way, because I'm a novelist, I realise that I'm one of the lucky ones. I can turn every negative experience into something positive.

My poor mother wasn't so lucky. It couldn't have been easy for her to leave her own home and go to live as a lodger in cramped digs. She had a strong sense of pride and dignity and the awful circumstances she sometimes found herself in must have been very hard to bear. She had great courage too, of course, which was just as well. I remember one time at the beginning of the war my father persuaded her to take Audley and me to Bathgate for safety from any air raids that might occur in Glasgow. She found a cottage and I can see it yet in my mind's eye. It was one-storey, tiny, low-roofed and white-walled. Inside was comprised of a shoebox-sized lobby with a bedroom leading off to the left and a living room to the right. A tiny scullery led off the living room.

As soon as we arrived and unpacked my mother took Audley across the road to visit our Auntie Jessie who lived in another cottage, behind stables if I remember correctly. All these buildings are long gone now. I was left in our cottage and I proceeded to get down on my knees and scrub the place from end to end. I even meticulously scrubbed all the skirting boards. I've no recollection of my mother asking me to clean the place. I honestly don't believe she'd do such a thing. Partly, I admit, because she wouldn't be that bothered about it. And anyway, it had looked clean enough to start with.

No, I think it more likely that this lone scrubbing incident was just an expression of the kind of obsessiveness that I eventually channelled into becoming a published writer.

Anyway, night came and my mother put cushions and blankets for Audley on the floor beside the double bed which she and I were to share. It was the only bed in the place. There was no electricity and after we were all settled, my mother blew out the candles. I was dozing off to sleep when I vaguely heard Audley cry out, 'Mummy, something bit me.'

My mother told him to go to sleep. But again he cried out that something had bitten him.

Eventually my mother got up and lit a candle. I was almost asleep again. I was so warm – even my head was hot and heavy as if something was pressing down on it. I remember my mother's urgent call to me, 'Margaret, don't move!'

It turned out that there was a rat on my head. Indeed the place was moving, seething with rats. My mother started throwing shoes about to chase them away. Audley and I got up and, bunched together, we moved into the lobby, throwing things and stamping noisily. Reaching the kitchen my mother went first and bombarded the place with everything she could get her hands on.

I heard her tell Auntie Jessie afterwards that the living room was heaving with rats.

There was no hot water in the house so we washed ourselves in cold water from the scullery tap. I washed my hair over and over again in the icy water.

I suppose we must have stayed up all night, I can't remember. Eventually we ended up in a room above a shoe shop. Then, because nothing was happening in Glasgow, we all moved back home. We were just in time, of course, for the start of the air raids.

There is a rich enough bank of emotion to draw from in that experience of being taken away with my mother or in the other experiences when I was left behind. There is enough to supply my needs for several novels. Not that one lifts experience straight from life. That would be reportage.

A creative artist doesn't copy life, he makes an arrangement of it to suit his own purpose. When Mrs Trollope was asked, 'Do you put real people in your books?' she replied, rather indelicately, 'Of course I draw from life, but I always pulp my acquaintances before serving them up. You would never recognise a pig in a sausage.' The writer is not concerned about whether it's a truthful likeness of the original characters or incidents – this would be inhibiting. The fiction writer wants to create a plausible harmony convenient to the story. For that, a writer has to be selective.

Alfred Hitchcock said that drama is real life with the dull bits cut out. One certainly has to keep this in mind when writing a novel.

But what one must put over honestly and accurately is the original feeling. The feeling need not necessarily spring from an incident in your own life, although it will probably be coloured by your own emotional experience. Novels are basically about people, and stories and story characters come into being by the writer observing and becoming moved or excited by facets of real-life people. The writer's imagination is excited and he or she is emotionally moved. As a result he or she feels compelled to communicate this excitement, this emotion, to the readers. *What the writer has felt at the beginning, the reader must feel at the end.*

I wish someone had told me this when I was writing my first novel. I just set to, not knowing anything. I produced an autobiographical, undisciplined (and, I suspect, self-pitying) splurge; a kind of shapeless outpouring. It must have been about the size of *Gone With The Wind* and it took a lot of tearing up and burning. This is what I eventually did with it.

With my next few books at least I made an attempt to tell a story. They were about wealthy people who lived in country mansions filled with priceless antiques. At that point in my life I had never met any wealthy people nor had I seen the inside of any country mansions. It might not have been so bad if I'd known how to do research but I'd never heard of research. I just conjured everything up out of my imagination.

8

It was years before it even occurred to me that anyone might actually want to buy my scribbles. After that it took quite a long while to save up to have what I'd written typed. Then there was all the time trying to find out where to send it. But I still persevered with writing whenever and wherever I got the chance.

At one time I was working in a shoe shop that shut for lunch. So I took sandwiches and determined that after the boss went home for her lunch I'd get out my novel and do a bit of work on it. I discovered, however, that once the doors were shut and the shop was quiet, an army of mice appeared. Nothing daunted, I took my piles of paper and a chair and sat in the doorway. This meant I was in full view of the street and causing quite a stir among passers-by. I managed to ignore these distractions. I couldn't ignore the boss's fury, however, when she returned to find people's attention more on a mess of papers in her doorway than the shoes in her window.

I was visiting a friend the other week and she was chatting about old times and she recalled one thing that I'd forgotten.

'I could never understand you when we were young, Margaret.'

'How's that?' I asked.

'Well, so often I'd say, "Come on, let's go to the dancing tonight." and you'd say, "I can't; I've got to stay in and write."'

Although of course I did get to the dancing sometimes and I met a young man and got married and had a baby.

By the time my son was three I was dragging him along the street to the nearest day nursery so that I could organise a few hours of writing. I really mean dragging, because the poor wee soul didn't want to go and screamed loudly and brokenheartedly. I feel distressed and guilty about doing this to him even now. In fact, quite recently I was feeling over-sensitive and this began to prey on my mind until I couldn't stand it any longer. I burst out to Kenneth (who is now a strapping six feet and a black belt in karate), 'I'm sorry for forcing you to go to that nursery, son. I've always regretted it, I knew I shouldn't have done it when it upset you so much.'

He rolled his eyes. 'For goodness sake, Mum! I'd forgotten all about that years ago.'

But I didn't feel any better until he'd given me one of his comforting bear hugs. Thinking of his time at the nursery brings back a painful reminder of an occasion when I neglected him. It was the time of the nursery Christmas party and all the children were going to be photographed with Santa. I was in the middle of a dreadfully stressful and distressing period in my second marriage and I suppose I couldn't cope. Anyway, I took Ken to the nursery that day with only his wee kilt and vest and a cardigan – no shirt. And the cardigan didn't even cover him properly because it had shrunk in the wash. I remember the nursery nurse looking at him, then looking at me in silent reproach. It seems incredible to me now that I did that to my wee boy. I keep asking myself even to this day – how could I have done that? Surely I had even a T-shirt I could have put on him. Even a dirty shirt would have been better than nothing. I grow cold inside thinking that he might have been cold. I still have the photograph of the group of children all dressed in their best party clothes grouped round Santa and poor wee Ken in his too-small cardigan with his vest showing. I sometimes wonder if he might have been bullied there too and, thinking that, I could die with guilt and worry and regret. But it does make me understand my mother a little better. No doubt there were times when she was in such a state in her marriage that she couldn't cope and that would explain the occasions when she neglected me.

I have always loved Ken. Maybe, after all, my mother always loved me. I keep trying to believe that.

My third novel, even looking back now, wasn't too bad. As I said, at least I was beginning to get the hang of technique. I was acquiring self-discipline in the actual handling and putting down of my material. I was learning how to be ruthless. I was spotting repetitions and slashing them out. It was beginning to occur to me that when I was anxious to put over some point or create some emotional response, I didn't succeed half so well if, in my anxiety to show how important it was, I went on and on about it (or had one of my characters go on and on about it).

It's strange but true that the more you pare down the words you use on these occasions (making sure of course that the words left are exactly the right words to convey your meaning precisely), the more punch the scene is likely to have. Characters spring to life more vividly too, emotion is more effectively aroused and your point gets straight home if your prose is not too long-winded, over-explanatory, repetitive, or cluttered with adjectives.

Sometimes I botched the writing in some other way and just had not succeeded in conveying to the reader the picture I had in my mind.

I remember, a lifetime ago, sending a story to a D. C. Thomson magazine. It was a story called *Flashpoint* about a character called Nancy. I got the story back with the following letter:

> Thank you for letting us see your story *Flashpoint* which I am now returning to you.
>
> You write very fluently but one essential point to bear in mind when writing for popular women's magazines is that

your main character must be likeable. Misguided, deluded or slow in the uptake are all permissible provided she is likeable with it. I felt what Nancy needed was a punch in the mouth!

That hurt at the time. I had thought Nancy *was* likeable. But after I recovered my equilibrium I read the story again. I discovered, to my surprise, that the Nancy on my typewritten pages was not at all the Nancy I thought I'd put there. She had changed during the journey from inside my head. I had failed in my intention.

It was my mother's burning ambition that I should get a story published in *The People's Friend* and I'm damned if I was able to do it. I tried and tried but somehow could never get the hang of it. My mother found this difficult to forgive. She certainly never understood.

'Such nice, simple wee stories,' she used to say. 'I'm sure you could write one if you tried.'

But I was determined to do whatever I could to get a novel published. I had always longed to be a novelist, not a short story writer. I think it was after I'd finished my fourth attempt at a novel that I saw an advert somewhere that criticism and revision to bring a book up to publishable standards could be done by experts at a price and I was hooked. I rushed my typescript away and was told by letter that it showed much promise and could be made publishable at a cost of £25. That was a lot of money in those days and it certainly was a fortune to me. I'd never had such a sum in my life. I determined to get it. I knew there was no use asking my parents. They didn't have that kind of money either. Anyway this was before I'd had a word published and the writing side of my life was never spoken of or in any way taken seriously by my family and friends. Success as a writer seemed within my grasp and by God I wasn't going to let it go.

In great fear and trepidation in case anyone saw me, I went to where a moneylender had an office in the main street in town. As I hovered outside the place trying to pluck up courage to enter, I was nearly dying of shame. But it was more than that. Looking back now, I realise that I was also shrinking from repeating a pattern of instinctual experience that had formed when I was a child.

Regular as clockwork every week, I was sent along to one or other of the local shops to ask, 'Could you please give me some butter and bread and tea and sugar and sausages and potatoes and chocolate biscuits?' And I was to tell whoever served me, 'My mammy will pay you at the end of the week.'

I knew instinctively as I set out for the shop that I was in charge of a vitally important errand. My 'antennae' had picked up the urgency from my mother, especially as she watched me from the window as I went along the road. Her back was as straight as ever and her head still had its proud tilt and she would smile and nod to me, encouraging me on. Yet I sensed her anxiety.

Entering the shop I would become lost in a forest of tall people but eventually would manage to crush a path towards a high wooden counter. Above it towered the shop assistant who seemed to always register disapproval and irritation at what I was going to say before I opened my mouth. I sensed looks being exchanged above my head. The boss appeared. The problem I had raised was discussed. Often customers joined in. In an agony of shame and suspense, I waited. If I was at last given the groceries it would be with a lecture about how they were giving them to me this time but if they didn't get paid by the end of the week, it would be the last time.

My anxiety was increased a hundredfold because I knew that they might not get paid at the end of the week. It might not be their turn and I would have to go back with some trumped up excuse that hadn't a chance of being believed. The complicated and fearful juggling game my mother played with money had to be seen to be believed. I don't know if my mother's grand, impulsive nature made my father insecure and overcautious and that's why he didn't give her much housekeeping money, or whether he was just being rotten. But I'll never forget the week my mother found that he had earned nine pounds and only given her three. (She had either rifled his pockets or read his diary. He never failed to record everything meticulously in his diary, no matter how often this habit was the means of bringing him to rough justice.)

Anyway, my mother, who seemed to live for the moment, would visibly relax when she spotted me tottering triumphantly along the road with a full basket of groceries. The whole atmosphere of the house would change. I would sense the air light and intoxicating the moment I stepped over the threshold. My mother would sing as she strode around making the dinner.

If by some awful chance I failed in my errand to the shops, the house would become as tight as a drum with anxiety and I would be sent off again to try another shop or, failing that, a neighbour or friend. It was better, though, if a shop saved the day because that meant chocolate biscuits.

Strange as it may seem this matter of the chocolate biscuits is important to me as a writer. It helps me to understand the apparently stupid, reckless, self-indulgent, spendthrift ways of some people who have been deprived. It's painful to be without the basic necessities and it does things not only to the body but to the spirit. There's the suspended anxiety, for instance, the shame that can't but must be faced of someone coming to the door when you've nothing to offer them, not even a cup of tea.

These are pains, these are anxieties that cause a wretched craving that, at the first opportunity, must be reassured and comforted away. What comforted my mother and me was chocolate biscuits. We really wolfed them whenever we got the chance.

It's an awful lot easier to keep an even keel and budget sensibly when at the same time you are secure in being able to continuously enjoy modest comforts and necessities. It was always a hunger and burst with us.

With nothing but this memory bank to draw on, my visit to the moneylender was an agony indeed. However, so strong was my desperation to succeed as a writer, I forced myself into the place. A man with certain Fagin-like features came to the counter and I told him in trembling voice how I needed £25 to get my novel published and would he please give it to me and I promised to pay it back as soon as I could.

He said to go home and ask my father.

So you see, there are decent and kindly moneylenders and I'll be forever grateful to that one. Not that I went home and asked my father. As I've said, I knew that was no use. I just went home and shut myself in the bathroom and had a tragic brokenhearted howl.

But I got over it and soon I was hard at work on my fifth novel.

It sounds easy saying it in one sentence like that. The truth is that time in the bathroom wasn't the only time I cried. I used to collapse over my notebooks and weep with sheer hopelessness and exhaustion. I used to think, 'I can't do it. It's just not in me to become a writer. No matter how hard I try I just haven't got the talent. There's no use pretending, I have to face the truth. I haven't got what it takes. I'll never do it.'

Then, from somewhere deep inside me would come a ripple of indignation and a 'thrawnness' as my mother would say. And I would suddenly sit up and think, 'No, damn it, I *will* do it! I will! If it takes me all my life, I'll get a book published – even if it happens the day before I die – I'll manage it!'

But I didn't manage it with my fifth book either.

'All right,' I thought, 'I'll change my tactics. Maybe I'm making the mistake of aiming too high to begin with. Maybe

I'm starting with something too big. Right, then. I'll try starting at the other end.'

So I wrote a letter to a women's magazine page and Hallelujah! I got it published! I'll never forget opening the magazine on the street (I couldn't wait until I got home) and there was my letter, my very own words, in print. A few days later I received a cheque for five pounds.

By this time my first marriage had ended and I had married again. My new husband was a widower with a young son and the letter was a heartfelt cry about the difficult situation of second wives and stepmothers. This happened to be the subject the magazine had asked for letters to be on that week.

About the same time I discovered that Glasgow Corporation ran a course on 'Literary Appreciation'. The man who took the course was a Mr Scoular and many a potential writer has gone through his hands and been grateful to him. The weekly meetings were held in a large hall, which was always packed. Mr Scoular would begin by giving a talk. All that I can remember of those was that in one he said that good journalism was when a paper said that ten thousand troops of the army in the USSR crossed the border of . . . at . . . Bad journalism was when the paper said that Red hordes had overrun . . .

After the talk he would read out an article or short story written by one of the audience. Then anyone in the audience who had an opinion about the piece would voice it. Finally, Mr Scoular gave his own views. I always thought his criticism was objective, constructive and fair. You had to be tough, however, to survive some of the things the audience said.

I had a friend who put in a story. It had quite a rough ride and she never wrote a story again in her life. This was a great pity because she had writing talent. To this day I can't mention Mr Scoular's name to her (and the poor man's dead and buried now) without her erupting in bitterness, hatred and resentment against him.

But my friend didn't fail to become a writer because of Mr Scoular or indeed anyone in that audience who said anything about her story. She has many excellent and indeed lovable personality traits. She just didn't have the right characteristics to be an author.

9

I plugged the stepmother–stepchild theme again in a story that I submitted to Mr Scoular's class.

It got a mixed reception at the class but the general consensus was that it was extremely moving. I now owned a typewriter and I typed a fresh copy and sent it winging its way to a glossy women's magazine. It came back with what I realise now was the most encouraging letter. To me, then, it was just another failure.

Perhaps, I thought, I was still aiming too high. I decided to organise an attack on D. C. Thomson's small magazines. First of all I bought them – *The People's Friend, Family Star, Red Letter, Secrets*, the lot. I read them from cover to cover and I hated them. I absolutely despised them. But I struggled with my emotions once I'd had a few of my stories returned from these same publications.

There was no use me slanging D. C. Thomson's stories. The fact was, I hadn't the expertise to write them.

I buckled down to make a serious study of each of the magazines. I even examined the advertising. Actually, this is important when doing market study. From the kind of advertising you can deduce what social class of reader the publication is aimed at, and what age group, and whether married or single; what kind of clothes are worn, what kind of jobs are held.

The problem pages and agony columns are also helpful not only for finding out the type of person who reads the magazine (and remember, the reader has to sympathise and identify with the story characters) but as a source of story ideas.

I gave the stories themselves my most concentrated attention. I analysed them, but not in the same way that stories were picked over and turned inside out and upside down in the classes I'd attended at the university extramural department. Now I was finding out practical, useful things like how the authors caught the reader's interest at the beginning of their stories (the interest hook), exactly how they sustained that interest (the conflict and the suspense) and how they ended the stories (the denouement, which had to be, for the most part, happy. Or at least hopeful or leaving the reader with the feeling – well, it was the best thing that could have happened in the circumstances.).

I analysed each story with a writer's eye – with the sole view of doing it myself.

I found that even with the romantic magazine stories, I had to approach the writing of them in much the same way as I would eventually approach the writing of a novel. Something would spark off an emotional response in me. I would feel amusement, resentment, pity, love, fear, anger, curiosity, compassion. Or I would observe emotions and tune into them in other people. Then I would shape this reaction or emotion into the form, the technique of the short story.

Most of the magazine short stories I studied were made up of a problem, conflict arising out of the problem, and the solution of the problem. With this in mind I wrote a story called *Waiting for the Crowdens*. I thought it might be the type that would appeal to *My Weekly*. It seemed to me that this magazine at that time specialised in quite good emotional-type stories and it was one of D. C. Thomson's publications which was aimed at older, married and more comfortably off readers.

The story spark came from an emotion aroused in me by my father-in-law. The old man had lived with us in worsening stages of senility since we'd been married. Sometimes he would be quite normal and capable. At other times, without warning, he would do awful things. Looking back I find some of them funny, although they were not quite so hilarious at the time. Like when I was trying to sell our house in Cardonald. I had put a very glowing advert in the paper about the house and a whole crowd of people came to see it. In my anxiety to make sure there were no hitches, I had worked like a slave scrubbing and polishing so that the place looked its best. Eventually I had about two dozen potential buyers crowded into my sitting room and I had been extolling the virtues of the house before showing them round, when suddenly my father-in-law shuffled in, rubbing his hands and announced to me, as if no one else were in the room, 'I'm away to the pub but I've left the electric fire on in my room to make it look as if it's warm!'

The next night I was leading a very prim and sedate couple upstairs to view the bedrooms when we were stopped in our tracks halfway by the vision of my father-in-law emerging from the bathroom in his shirt-tails and carrying a chamber pot.

'Evening!' he said and carried on upstairs. I had no option but to follow him with the now horrified lady and gentleman in tow.

It took a long time to sell that perfectly good house but I eventually managed it and at nearly 100 per cent profit.

But to get back to *Waiting for the Crowdens*. I was expecting friends for a meal and wanted to give them a nice evening. But the problem was my father-in-law, who always ate with us and who was now dropping his food all over the table and slavering and generally making a terrible mess. The poor soul couldn't help it. I realised that and I think I can truthfully say that I never once criticised him about this or complained to him or indeed ever said an unkind word to him – certainly not that I'm aware of. But it could make one feel physically sick at times. It could also be excruciatingly embarrassing when guests were in. So when I was expecting these particular guests, who had never been to our house before, I found myself in a dilemma. It's a long time ago now and I can't remember exactly, but I suppose I wanted to impress them and I was afraid my father-in-law would show me up.

After much nailbiting, worry and indecision, I eventually gave him his meal in his room. I felt horribly guilty about it. Although looking back now I can see I had absolutely no need. The old man and I got on well and I nursed him as best I could through thick and thin for years before he died. I did feel distraught and guilty about giving him his dinner in his room and, when I came to write *Waiting for the Crowdens*, I decided to use this emotion and to base the story on this incident.

Now we come to the technique bit.

During the telling of a short story, either the situation in which the characters are placed undergoes a change, or the characters adapt to fit the situation. In either case, something must change. If no change occurs, then it is a sketch not a story. A short story deals with a particular incident, a brief space of time in the life of a character. It highlights one small but telling part. It illuminates rather than develops. (A novel develops.) So, keeping all these things I've said about the short story in mind, I set to thinking of how I could adapt the real-life emotion, characters and situation to the medium of the short story.

First, I thought of how the closer the relationship of the character was, the stronger the story drama was likely to be. So I thought – right, a father/daughter relationship is closer than a father-in-law/daughter-in-law relationship. So that's what I'll make it. Then it occurred to me that it might be even better, especially for a women's magazine, to make it a mother rather than a father. So it became a mother in my mind. So, it was going to be a story about a woman – let's call her Moira – who is expecting people to dinner and her mother is going to create a problem.

Now, here's another part of technique I had to remember, and this applies to the novel as well as the short story. I had to make the most of every situation. And push everyone to their limits. So instead of making it just any old dinner, for instance, I made it a Christmas dinner. You can see immediately how this strengthens the dilemma and enables me to make the most of the emotions involved.

Now I've got to think of the characters in more detail. I've got to get their motivations clear in my mind. Instead of making Moira just a harassed housewife, instead of making her just a little embarrassed, I push her into much stronger emotions.

I begin my story by stating the problem in the first sentence. I set the scene, at the same time revealing Moira's character. Then, to keep up the suspense as well as feeding in more information, I go into flashback. I don't make the ending exactly what you'd call a happy one but it is as it should be – that is, it is intended to make the reader feel: Yes, that is the best that could have happened in the circumstances.

That story eventually turned out to be one of the most successful I ever wrote and earned me a tidy sum.

10

I had many short stories published after that and in all sorts of styles – romantic, humorous, crime, literary – and I had quite a few broadcast. But how can I tell you of the joy I felt when I had that first story accepted? It wasn't the sight of my words in print or hearing them read by an actress on radio. Although these things were thrilling enough.

I'd done it. I'd cracked it. I'd shown them. I'd won!

Yet it was more than that. I had such a desperate need to reach out to someone. Looking back, I now realise that I'd always had this need even as, indeed especially as, a young child. It had taken root then in terror and insecurity and in a desperate need for help.

John Steinbeck said:

A writer out of loneliness is trying to communicate like a distant star sending signals. He isn't telling or teaching or ordering. Rather he seeks to establish a relationship of meaning, of feeling, of observing.

We are lonesome animals. We spend all our life trying to be less lonesome. One of our ancient methods is to tell a story begging the listener to say – or feel – 'Yes, that's the way it is, or at least that's the way I feel it. You're not as lonely as you thought.'

I determined to consolidate my success. I'd get a story into every magazine I aimed for – even if it was just the once – just to prove to myself that I could do it. So I tried other D. C. Thomson magazines and I got other stories published in them, before moving on to bigger publications. But don't imagine I simply sent in stories after that and got them accepted. It's never that easy. I sent in stories and I got them back. Time after time after time. What kept me going now was the belief that if I had done it once I could do it again.

A whole new world of possibilities began to open up before me and in more ways than one.

It was D. C. Thomson's policy after they bought a few stories from you, having established a working relationship, to invite you to meetings with their editors. An editor would come up to Glasgow, for instance, and from his hotel base, he would invite an author to morning coffee, another for afternoon tea. The more established you were, the more lavish the hospitality offered. You graduated from coffee and biscuits, to afternoon tea and sandwiches, to lunch, and then to dinner. The highest accolade was when you were invited to come through to Dundee to be shown around their offices and meet all their editors. You were booked in at a hotel and had dinner, and breakfast, and morning coffee and lunch and afternoon tea. The whole works!

At Christmas they sent you a tartan tin of shortbread.

I was still at the morning coffee stage when I was told by letter that they were starting a new magazine – a glossy-type magazine – and the editor of it wished to meet me to discuss the contribution I could make. This was terribly exciting. To be in at the beginning of a new magazine – a big, glossy magazine! But, as I've said before, it's never easy to get a story accepted. Failure was the constant spectre at my elbow. Determined to succeed, however, I set off early for the hotel armed with my pencil and notebook to jot down every pearl of wisdom that fell from the editor's lips. It wasn't so much what to do that I had to find out. With D. C. Thomson it was more important to know what *not* to do.

No doubt they are different now. But at that time they

were a funny firm. They had these strict taboos they couldn't bring themselves to lay on the line. You had the most awful job to find out, and usually only did so by trial and error; for instance, no story in which the heroine smoked a cigarette was ever accepted. Drink was definitely not on. And you risked doing yourself a professional injury with kissing and canoodling.

Of course, for all I knew, they might be breaking new ground with this latest magazine. It was imperative for me to find out. I arrived too early for my appointment and sat with notebook on knee and pen poised at the ready. I was slightly nonplussed when the editor eventually arrived. Instead of the usual father-type figure, he was a comparatively young and rather attractive man. Quickly recovering, however, I got straight down to business.

'About sex,' I burst out, 'how far can I go?'

His eyes twinkled. 'How far do you want to go, love?'

It didn't even occur to me to smile. I just pressed earnestly on with my enquiries. I've always taken my job as a writer very seriously.

It turned out that they wanted emotional stories for that magazine exactly of the type I had been writing for *My Weekly* and BBC Radio. This suited me fine. I'd written lots of other types by now (and not only for D. C. Thomson); you name it, I'd had a go at it. But I preferred the serious emotional kind.

The funny thing was, though, by this time my personal life was going through a ghastly phase and I'm damned if I could write anything but either suspense thrillers or humour. There is an interesting point here. Just think of all the clowns and comedians who have suffered from depression or committed suicide. I've come to the conclusion that you can only make use of the really harrowing stuff in retrospect – once you're safely removed from the intimate personal experience of it.

Wordsworth no doubt realised it too when he spoke of

poetry being an overflow of powerful feelings but added:

> It takes its origin from emotion recollected in tranquillity: the emotion is contemplated till, by a species of reaction, the tranquillity gradually disappears and an emotion, kindred to that which was before the subject of contemplation, is gradually produced, and does itself actually exist in the mind.

That can be difficult and harrowing enough, but from a retrospective situation at least you're working from a position of safety and physical strength. It's like being in the centre of a whirlpool or a tornado. It's possible to conjure up a vivid and exciting description of it long afterwards when you're sitting in the quiet safety of your room. At the time of being in the whirlpool or the tornado all you can do is struggle to survive.

I was struggling with my father-in-law, who by this time was doing things like trying to set the house on fire in the middle of the night. He seemed to be all right when my husband was in during the day (although my husband at that time went out quite a lot with his friends during the day so he didn't really see all that much of his father). At night when my husband was out working as a taxi driver, the old man completely lost not only his mind but also control of his bladder and bowels. Every evening he disintegrated as a human being. I had to continuously struggle to lift him and lay him. He used to fall out of bed, fall from his chair in front of the fire, fall downstairs, get outside wearing only his pyjamas and fall in the street.

Apart from the physical toll it took out of me, I became very depressed. It was so sad to look at the photograph on the wall of the handsome young man the old man had once been and to witness his terrible disintegration. Fortunately, he didn't seem to know about it. He used to chat away quite happily (and loudly) in the middle of the night to friends long dead. Sometimes he'd get angry with them and shout at me to take them away. But next morning he never remembered anything about it.

Perhaps it was understandable that my husband never believed me that anything was wrong. All the same, our marriage began to deteriorate and not only because of the strains imposed by my father-in-law. No doubt I was as much to blame as my husband. As I said to my mother, there are two sides to every story. I couldn't stand some of his friends. He couldn't stand my mother. She couldn't stand him – though eventually they became friends and he was kind to her and she became quite fond of him. But I was drained, both physically and emotionally. I took a heart attack and then I had to go to hospital for an operation.

When I returned home and buckled down to write that serious emotional story for the new magazine, I just couldn't do it. I found myself writing a light-hearted piece of nonsense. It was a very long time before I could tackle a serious story again.

When I did, I wrote a story about an old man dying. Another very successful one was about a woman who has left her husband and is wandering the streets of Glasgow with her children, trying to find a place to live. A third, which was published in this country and several countries overseas and was also given repeat broadcasts, was about a woman who was faced with the decision of bringing her mother, who was in need of care, to live with her or putting her into an institution.

I'd now had a great many short stories published. My real goal in life, however, had always been and still was to become a novelist. I didn't regret my time writing short stories. I regarded it as my apprenticeship as a writer. And it had bolstered my sagging confidence. Now I was able to spur myself on by repeating to myself that if I could get short work into print, I could get long work into print. It was just a matter of sticking at it and learning the appropriate techniques.

With this in mind, I travelled down to Derbyshire to attend my first Writers' School at the Hayes Conference Centre in Swanwick. This is where I met my dear wee friend John Maloney.

I can still see him hirpling about excitedly (he had a club foot) among all the writers in that beautiful place.

I was overcome with hysterical excitement myself. Here, at last, I was among my own kind. Here were writers – 300 of them, all bursting to talk about writing. Gloriously, gloriously happy times! I've gone every year since with the same delirious happy excitement but now at least I don't leave at the end of the week with my face red and swollen after tearful goodbyes to so many dearly loved friends. I know that I will be able to see many of them quite often at other places during the year, as well as every year at Swanwick.

That first year, one of the lecturers was Alexander Cordell. I was so moved by his lecture and the excerpts he read from one of his books that afterwards I left the lecture hall and went straight to my bedroom and wept with – I don't know – the sheer emotional appreciation of it all.

Later, outside on the sunny lawn, I plucked up the courage to approach Cordell. I spilled out all my troubles (everyone does this to everyone all the time at Swanwick), about how I'd written five novels and none of them were any use and how I desperately wanted to write books that would get published.

True to what I now know is the Swanwick tradition, he gave me his help and advice in a most generous and unstinting way. At one point in our conversation he asked, 'Where are you from, Margaret?'

'Glasgow,' I said.

Then he asked what kind of background I had had, what kind of environment.

'Oh, nothing interesting,' I said. 'Just the Glasgow tenements.'

'Well,' he said, 'my advice to you is to go back from Swanwick and sit down and, with as much courage and honesty as you can muster, write a novel about life in the Glasgow tenements.'

I stared at him in astonishment. It had never occurred to me to do that.

11

On my way home from Swanwick I closed my eyes and drifted back to the jungle of Glasgow streets.

For some time now I'd been living in a middle- to upper-middle-class place outside Glasgow, called Bearsden. There were no Glasgow-type tenements there. People lived in roomy terraced houses (our terraced house had six rooms and also a kitchen big enough to eat in and a scullery and a bathroom) or neat bungalows or large villas. The streets were lined with trees and within minutes you could be away by car to beautiful countryside. Everybody had a car. There was a car park – thickly screened by trees – at the back of the shops in the centre of Bearsden. The centre was referred to as 'The Village' and we lived just along from the shops.

I had never seen a housewife going about her business in that place looking harassed. They all seemed so well fed, so well dressed, so sure of themselves in their comfortable routines. Their lives (or so it appeared) were a continuous round of coffee mornings during which they admired each other's home baking and swapped recipes, or managed to keep them secret. Somebody's new curtains were noted and criticised. The previous day's golf or evening's bridge was verbally replayed. The merits and demerits of new fashions in clothes or furnishings were argued about. Keep-fit efforts, slimming failures and successes were giggled at or sighed over. Diets were discussed eagerly and *endlessly*.

It seemed to me at the time, perhaps mistakenly, that looking after oneself and cushioning oneself from any disturbing ripples in life had been mastered by many to a fine art. The main object in existence (by some, but of course not all), it seemed to me – apart from looking after oneself – was to keep up appearances and to be seen to fit in to the accepted patterns and conventions. This view of Bearsden and the people living there could have been unfairly coloured by my acute unhappiness at the time and my lack of self-confidence in communicating properly with anyone.

I eventually wrote a book called *The Prisoner* which I set in Bearsden and in which I delve beneath the surface appearances of respectability. Of this book one reviewer said many complimentary things but ended by remarking, 'I don't know what they'll think of it in Bearsden though!'

I didn't wait to find out. But I'm jumping the gun.

I must return to that train journey from Swanwick. There I was, allowing myself to drift back in time to life in the Glasgow I'd once known. As I did so, I 'tuned in' more and more to the feelings, to the essence of the place and to the people who had lived there. At first vague images of people and scenes floated into my head. Gradually I began to feel my way into them. I concentrated my senses on them.

I heard children singing and playing in the streets. The sound of their peever scraped close to my ear. Their ball thumped rhythmically.

'One-two-three-a-leary, four-five-six-a-leary, seven-eight-nine-a-leary, ten-a-leary postman!'

Women puffed and hustled along, each clutching a shopping bag heavy as a sack of coal in one hand and a purse in the other. Groups of women laughed and enjoyed a good blether in shops, in close mouths (tunnel-like entrances to tenement buildings) or at street corners. Coal horses clopped along led by black-faced coalmen bawling, 'Co-o-ee, any o-o-ee fo-o-ee! Co-o-ee!'

I smelled kippers cooking, and sausages.

The close was draughty and had a damp chill as I entered it and went skipping up the stairs. A symphony of sounds whirled around me. From behind closed and open doors came laughter and angry shouting.

'Wullie! If you don't stop tormentin' that wean, ah'm gonnae murder ye!'

My mother played 'The Old Rugged Cross' on the piano. Alvar Liddell was on the wireless telling everyone the news. Someone was jauntily singing, 'All the nice girls love a sailor, all the nice girls love a tar, tum – tee – tum – tee – tum – tee – tum, tum – tee – tum – tee – tum – tee – tum – Ship ahoy! Ship ahoy!'

Despite the cold winter's air, the warm, crowded, cheery bustle of it all . . .

The more I concentrated on it, the more intensely I felt it. I felt it in my bones. But how to make a novel of it? Where did I start? During the next few days and weeks I gave my thoughts and instincts free rein. I also went back and wandered about the streets I'd once known so well.

My mother and father still lived in the same corporation housing scheme in Balornock, although not in the same flat. My brother, now married to his childhood sweetheart, lived down the hill in a room and kitchen in Springburn. My aunt and uncle and cousins also lived in a room and kitchen in an old tenement in Springburn and their lavatory was also out on the landing. This tiny windowless and lightless lavatory had to be shared by several other families and if you weren't very nippy on your feet it wasn't always easy to get in there. If nature called and the place was engaged there just had to be some other way to relieve the problem.

My Aunt Meg had what she called 'the Throne'. In the front room there was a walk-in cupboard which had a curtain instead of a door. In the cupboard, as well as everything from old paint brushes to old mattresses, there was a zinc pail. This was what my aunt referred to when she told me kindly, 'Don't worry, hen. Just away through and use the Throne!'

She suffered terribly with asthma and had to puff up and down the stairs to empty the pail when she could catch the lavatory at a vacant moment (which was probably only in the middle of the night).

I never heard her complain about that or anything. In fact she was always saying how lucky she was having the Co-op so handy at the corner. Her neighbours, she insisted, were absolute 'gems'. If she wasn't well, or if she needed a loan of a wee drop sugar, all she had to do was knock on the wall of her kitchen cupboard and Nelly from the next close would hear her and come to the rescue.

Aunt Meg had a pawky sense of humour that was only bettered by my Uncle Dode's hilarious one. He was my mother's brother and he had her marvellous spirit. Even after he went blind, he could keep you in stitches. His health steadily deteriorated but I remember my mother and I, on our way to visit him, met the doctor coming out of my uncle's house. By this time, as I say, Uncle Dode was blind and in pain yet the doctor, as he emerged from the house, was laughing.

'I felt really depressed before I went in there,' he told my mother, 'but he always manages to cheer me up!'

When my uncle was lying on his deathbed and my parents and I went to see him, my father sighed and said, 'The last time we met, Dode, I was the one who was ill and you were visiting me.'

'Aye, Sam,' my uncle managed, 'but when I came to see you I brought you a bottle of whisky.'

It was strange, looking back, how I remembered so much laughter. The poorer, the more distressing the circumstances, the stronger the sense of humour there seemed to be. There was a strong sense of community too, family feelings of loyalty and compassion and the recognition of responsibility to help one another that spilled far beyond one's immediate family. I wasn't idealising or being sentimental about the people and the background. I was looking back with a clear and honest eye. In my experience, that is how the people were.

I remember, for instance, the McLellands downstairs from us. They had a big family and Mr McLelland (through no fault of his own) was unemployed. One time when my father was on night shift a burglar tried to get in our door. My mother banged on the floor with a poker. It wakened Mr McLelland and, taking it as a sign that help was needed, he never even stopped to put on his trousers. He rushed upstairs in his shirt-tails to see what was wrong. On learning from my mother that the man he had passed on the stairs had tried to break into our house, Mr McLelland turned tail and raced after him. I was only a child at the time and I recall with perfect clarity watching out of the front room window and seeing Mr McLelland's half naked body and long hairy legs flying along the road in pursuit of his quarry. He punched the living daylights out of him when he caught him.

Eventually the McLellands couldn't pay their rent and had to 'do a moonlight'. The coalman or someone had loaned them a horse and cart. They piled the cart as best they could with all their worldly possessions. Then they climbed on top and the whole thing trundled away.

There was at that time what was known as 'the back road to Auchinairn'. It was hardly more than a lane and it ran between the hospital mortuary and some high bushes, behind which were fields and a few derelict farm buildings. It was in one of these buildings – probably an old barn – that the McLellands sought shelter. After that, their old neighbours, including my mother, used to take turns about every week to walk to the back road with a jug of soup or whatever they could manage to scrape up. I remember my mother taking me with her one night and Mrs McLelland coming to the door in her nightdress. She was carrying a lantern. I'll never forget how ill she looked and how her nightdress billowed out in the cold wind. And I had the impression of the children somewhere in the darkness behind her. I was only a child myself but I felt instinctively the terrible deprivation the family must have been suffering there. Mrs McLelland died soon afterwards, of malnutrition it was said. Not long after her death her son Robert was taken to the infirmary. He was about my age, perhaps a little younger. What I remember about him is his pale delicate face, his sad eyes and his too-big 'parish' jacket and trousers. Even after all these years his face floats before my mind's eye like a ghost. My mother and I visited him regularly and he always used to cling on to the neck of her blouse. She would cradle him in her arms and nurse him like a baby.

One day he asked her, 'Mrs Thomson, am I going to die?'

The doctor had already told my mother that although the appendectomy had been successful, the child was so undernourished he hadn't the strength to survive.

My mother said, 'Don't worry, son. All it means is you'll be seeing your mammy again.'

He did die and there seemed no doubt that his death was caused by malnutrition. It seems incredible that within living memory such things could happen. But they did.

I remember everything – the laughter and the tears. But I was still groping with how best to fashion my material into a novel.

Eventually I got down to business. I got myself organised with main characters. I chose characters that were as different to one another as possible. Contrast and conflict are essential. Even in his earliest days, Sir Walter Scott realised this:

> When I was a child, indeed for some years after, my amusement was in supposing to myself a set of persons engaged in various scenes which contrasted them with each other, and I remember to this day the accuracy with which my childish imagination worked.

Conflict has to be engendered because without conflict there's no story. I also kept in mind what I had learned from my short story writing. Clashes and episodes are always more striking when they happen among relatives or close friends and lovers. I also knew by this time that conflict was achieved by creating an important desire or requirement and putting in the way of its accomplishment all the obstruction you can reasonably introduce. You had to make sure that characters were truly trapped in the conflict, that being the type of people they were, no alternatives were open to them.

So I had to think of characters and conflict. I also had to decide when – in exactly what year – my story would start and exactly where it would be set. I knew it was going to be set in the city of Glasgow but where in Glasgow? In what street? In what house? And why?

It's not possible to say what you think of first and what second, and so on. You're just thinking about everything all the time and everything gradually becomes clearer and falls into place. At the same time, it becomes more complicated and you have to start taking voluminous notes. Let me explain.

Once I decided to start my story in 1936, I had to check in the local reference library what was going on not only in Glasgow, but in the world in general in 1936. (This was my first attempt at research, something else I had learned at Swanwick.) Not everything in the world, you understand, just the things that my characters would know about or be interested in. What they would know most about and be most interested in of course would be what was going on and what affected them in their own city. One way I found out what was going on was by reading newspapers of the time. Once you start doing a bit of research like this, one thing leads to another and it's amazing how what you discover helps with your character building and plotting. For instance, I discovered (or was reminded) that the big things in Glasgow every year were:

1. the Govan Fair; 2. the Orange Walk; 3. the Glasgow Fair fortnight.

As I read first of all about the Govan Fair I was intrigued by the history of it and the vivid images it brought to mind, the pageantry, the decorated floats, the crowds, the excitement. I began to feel myself into it. I became one of the people there. No, not only one, I flitted about inside different people – men, women and children. I was up there on one of the floats waving down at the crowd. I was crushing and jumping among the crowd, cheering and waving back.

I was away. This was it. The book was taking life. But wait. I had been told at Swanwick that it was a good idea to start a book just before a big event. So I decided to start my book in Govan (a district of Glasgow) just before the annual fair, in the middle of my characters' preparations for it.

But what characters?

Now I come to what is for me the most important part of creative writing.

12

According to Proust, characterisation was the breaking down of observed people and the putting together again. From the breakdown of one observed character, you can put together at least a dozen fictional characters, each of whom is different from the other. You take one main characteristic (more if necessary – there can be no hard and fast rules) and you exaggerate that, and to it you add other, different characteristics, some perhaps from another observed character, some chosen from your imagination to strengthen the impression you want to create. An important purpose of characterisation is to make the reader feel strongly in a specific way towards the person whom you are characterising.

Scott drew a bitter portrait of his father in one book and a pleasanter one in another. Stendhal, in one of his manuscripts, noted the names of the persons who had suggested his characters. Dickens portrayed his father in Mr Micawber, and Leigh Hunt in Harold Skimpole. Turgenev stated that he could not create a character at all unless as a starting point he could fix his imagination on a living person. And he said that it is only if you have a definite person in your mind that you can give vitality and idiosyncrasy to your own creation.

But the writer does not copy the originals. Copying isn't creating. The writer takes what he wants from people. He takes a few traits that have caught his attention, a turn of mind that has interested him and fired his imagination, something that has aroused his feelings. It's often enough for him to have caught a glimpse of someone in a railway station or chatted to him for a few minutes at a party. He only needs that tiny fertile substratum. He can build on it using his own experience of life, his knowledge of human nature and his intuition.

Everyone is affected by joy, fear, love and hate. Everyone is attached to his own opinions. Everyone has an infinite quality of mercy for his own failings and weaknesses. Each fictional character must have something of these contradictions to appear original and true to life. Only by opposites in character can drama be drawn and suspense created, only by a clash of wills can character develop and demonstrate itself.

I mulled over character creation. Already, seething noisily, rumbustiously around me (in my imagination) were the people of the Glasgow tenements as I had known them. Not people with faces that I'd ever seen. But people I sensed I knew from the inside.

But I had to have main characters, and one in particular with whom the reader could continuously identify.

I bought myself some school jotters and in front of the first one I wrote (after long and painful thought and studying of telephone directories): CATRIONA MUNRO.

Inside the jotter I made a list which ran like this:

Name: Catriona Munro
Address:
Age at beginning of story:
Height:
Weight:
Colouring: Hair
          Complexion
          Eyes
Physical characteristics and general description:
Mannerisms:
What kind of clothes does she wear?
What kind of food does she eat?

Does she drink and/or smoke? (If so, what?)
Background and home life:
Main personality traits (good and bad):

Once I'd filled in my character's name I then came to her address and was forced to start imagining her setting. I thought of my own home when I was a girl in Balornock. I remembered the narrow strip of kitchenette with its two inconveniently high shelves. There were no kitchen units in those days to keep everything dust and fly free. At least, not for us. My mother used to keep food in the only thing in the kitchenette that had a door on it – the oven. There was a wooden chair jammed in between the zinc boiler and the coal bunker. I used to sit there and have my breakfast off the top of the boiler before going to school or work. My mother and father slept on a bed settee in the living room where we usually ate. It was a small room and at night the table and chairs had to be jammed back so that the settee could be opened and the bed made ready. I slept on a bed settee in the front room (which meant I couldn't go to bed early if my mother had visitors in). My young brother slept in the bedroom. That was when we had the downstairs flat.

Upstairs lived Mrs Davidson, a mountain of a woman who liked nothing better than to sit at her front room window watching the world go by, at the same time making comments about it. Some of these were quite scathing, like when she saw one man passing and remarked, 'Look at that lazy sod. He's never done a stroke of work since he's retired!'

Our front room, like our living room, might have been depressingly shabby and drab had it not been for the colourful riot of Christmas cards, toffee tins and biscuit tins decorating every available surface. My mother liked a pretty picture and if it happened to be on a Christmas card or a toffee tin, she saw no reason why it should not give her (and, she firmly believed, everyone else who entered her house) continuing pleasure. We never took our Christmas cards down.

Embarrassed by this eccentricity, I used to make desperate attempts to remove them before one of my friends arrived. But in a clash of wills with my mother there was seldom any doubt as to who would come out victorious. My mother had a strong independent spirit and as she often said, would bend the knee to no one.

'Even if the Queen walked in that door,' she used to say, 'I wouldn't bend the knee to her. I'd just treat her the same as any other decent body.'

Thinking of my mother really took me back. I didn't just see that house in my imagination, I was there again. I was plunged into the gloom of the windowless lobby. The draught was rattling the letterbox. I could hear my father's voice raised in heated argument about politics with another dungareed railwayman in the living room. In the front room my mother was sitting at the piano, chin up, chest heaving in a rendering of 'If I can help somebody, as I go along. If I can help somebody with a word or song . . .'

My brother Audley was sitting on the chair in the kitchenette reading and getting the heat from the gas cooker.

I decided to make Catriona Munro's home a bottom flat in a tenement, but not in Balornock, which was on the north side of the city. It was more convenient for the purpose of my story if she lived over the Govan side. I thought up an imaginary place called Farmbank, which I visualised as a sort of extension of Govan – a corporation housing scheme tacked on to the Govan conurbation of very much older tenements around the shipyards. (I realise now that I didn't need to make it a fictitious place. I could quite easily have used a real place – somewhere over that end of the city.)

I broke off from filling up the notebook about Catriona's character to start another notebook about Farmbank. I drew a street map of the place and wrote in imaginary names of streets. I pinpointed Catriona's street and close and flat. On a separate page I drew a map of the house. (By the way, in Scotland flats are referred to as houses.)

My imagination had taken over. I was creating something and this process continued. I wasn't drawing or describing my old home in Balornock. This was Catriona Munro's home in Farmbank; I could make it, and its furnishings, and its occupants *any way I liked.* Can there be any thrill to match it, this God-like freedom of the mind and spirit?

Soon I knew number 10 Fyffe Street as well as, if not better than, I knew the flat in Balornock. I knew where every light switch was. I knew every crack in every ceiling. I knew much more than I would ever need to put in any book. And this is how it should be.

There are times now when I try to remember my Balornock home and I find I get quite confused. The Farmbank one is still so real to me.

I was able to fill in Catriona's address. The next thing to consider was what age she had to be at the beginning of the story. One had to be careful about the war. For one thing, the chances were the Govan Fair was not held during the war. So many people would be away in the armed forces. It occurred to me at this point that a lot of good emotional stuff could be found in the war years. So it would be a good idea to bring them in later.

This reminds me of a characteristic a novelist has that I haven't yet touched on. It's as if there are two people inside a writer's skin. Flaubert believed that he was, quite literally, two different persons. (Actually there are lots of people but there are two *main* ones.) For instance, a novelist could be grieving, and grieving sincerely at the death of a loved one, but at the same time, inside, would be observing, with curious detachment, the event and every reaction to it; filing everything away to be used if necessary in some future story. Always, all the time, the writer is looking with that cool, curious eye over his or her shoulder.

I plumped eventually for 1936, when I reckoned Catriona ought to be sixteen. Then came her description. I thought for a while about that and gradually filled in all the details – one detail somehow leading smoothly and naturally to another. She had long, fair hair and was small and frail. She was timid and soft-spoken. She was dominated by her mother.

Now, in every character there must be part of yourself. And there is something of me in Catriona. But Catriona is not me. (For one thing, I wasn't as old as sixteen in 1936!) I don't look like her. I had worked at about twenty different jobs before getting married. I was timid, yes. But I was a lot of other things as well. There were times when I could fight back tooth and nail and I always had this strong, persevering spirit.

But I only needed to take one real characteristic and exaggerate that and I only needed the essence of experience.

While I was filling the first jotter with every detail of Catriona, I had to probe into her background. That meant thinking about her parents. So before I knew where I was, my next two characters were being born.

Soon I was filling in their details in other notebooks. Soon I knew everything there was to know about Hannah and Rab Munro. As I saw, one thing leads to another and when I was filling in details about Rab, I had to think about where he would work. I gave this a lot of serious thought. I wanted for the unity and convenience of my story to have a nucleus – a central point where all my characters could meet. From my long apprenticeship in writing, I instinctively knew that it would be technically and artistically viable to have the unity of a central core. I felt a need for order. Right from the start, too, I felt a need to portray the character of Glasgow.

Gradually the thought of a corner shop wafted into my mind. Impressions and sensations of innumerable corner shops I'd known crowded in on me. And what better than a baker's shop as well as a general store? Yes, yes, with a bakehouse at the back. That way I could have a central scene for action day and night.

Then it suddenly came to me – Rab is one of the bakers. The bakers are my characters. The bakers and their families. In fact I would call the book *The Breadmakers*. They could all live in the flats above the bakery. All, that is, except Rab. I couldn't let him live there because if I was going to have Catriona my main character, then it was she who must work out her destiny there. It surely would be too inhibiting for her (and me, the author) to have her mother and father living there as well. Anyway, I'd already established that Catriona, Rab and Hannah lived in Farmbank.

So how does Catriona get from Farmbank to – I broke off to start yet another notebook, to draw maps of Govan and the imaginary streets and bakehouse and shop and all the crush of tenement buildings around it. I eventually called the street Dessie Street. So how does Catriona get to Dessie Street?

But first I had to do research on bakers and bakehouses. I'd never known a baker in my life and I'd never set foot in a bakehouse.

13

It was strange, but despite the fact that I could now claim to be a published writer I still hadn't the *belief* that I was a writer. After all, I wasn't a novelist. I hadn't the necessary proof that I was a novelist. That is, I couldn't say that I'd had a book published. So when I went into a baker's shop to ask if I could speak to a baker about his job, I felt acutely shy and completely lacking in self-confidence.

I hung away at the back of a crowd of customers until an assistant, spotting me despite my nervous shrinking, called over, 'Can I help you?'

My urgent reason for being there stuck in my throat. I felt ashamed and embarrassed. In an effort to appear perfectly normal I asked for half a dozen crumpets. While the assistant was putting them into a paper bag, I feverishly rehearsed what I had really come to say. But when I found I was being fixed with a gaze of enquiry and encouraged with the words, 'Yes? Was there something else?' I replied, 'Two rhubarb tarts and a small brown loaf.'

Eventually, after I'd bought enough cakes and scones and bread to last me all week, I blurted out in desperation, 'I'm a writer. I'm writing a book about bakers. Is there a baker here who would help me?' (Is there a baker in the house!)

To my surprise I found the assistant – all the assistants were thrilled. They'd never met a writer before. They dashed into the nether regions of the shop and reappeared after a while with an elderly man who looked as if he'd changed into his best suit and slicked down his hair. He seemed pleased and flattered to have someone interested in him and his job. He, it turned out, was the master baker and the owner of the premises. (What could be better? I immediately decided to have an old master baker in my book and he could own the shop and bakehouse in Dessie Street. In fact, why not make him own the tenement building? That way the bakers in his employ who lived in the flats above would be in 'tied houses'. I might get a bit of extra drama and conflict out of that.)

I had come prepared with a few basic questions in my notebook. But of course, not knowing anything about the subject, I didn't really know what to ask. However, I encouraged the old man to talk freely about his job and I listened with interest. The questions, or the initial lack of them, turned out to be no problem. Questions arose out of what he was telling me. As well as being my first experience of doing research with a person rather than just books, this was also my first lesson in interviewing people. I have found people invariably helpful and eager to talk about themselves. The secret is to allow them, to encourage them to talk freely. You should never on these occasions impose your own personality, opinions or views on the conversation. You should never sit in judgement on the other person. You should acquire the art of listening with sympathy and understanding and an open mind – the novelist's mind.

Lionel Trilling said that the novel was the literary form to which the emotions of understanding and forgiveness were indigenous, as if by the definition of the form itself.

Sometimes, however, the most difficult part of interviewing someone is to keep a straight face. I well remember one Glasgow woman getting quite carried away about her blackguard of a husband.

'He's a right rotten pig, so he is,' she hotly insisted. 'I just have nothin' to dae wi' him!'

77

I couldn't help feeling somewhat bewildered.

'I don't quite understand,' I ventured mildly. 'I mean, you do have seven children.'

She was nonplussed. But only for a moment.

'Aye . . . eh . . . aye . . . but I'm an awful heavy sleeper!'

The old master baker also got quite carried away. I was in his company for hours. There was nothing he didn't tell me about bakers and baking. I even learned that there were particular diseases that bakers were prone to like bronchitis and dermatitis. They tended to go bald as well. I later double-checked all this from other sources and as I began to get a picture of the lives of these men (remember I'm talking about 1936 – that was the time about which I was researching), I also began to get a picture of my 'Breadmakers'. Soon I had, as well as my old master baker Duncan McNair, his son Melvin, who was determined to keep fit and avoid these diseases.

Poor Rab Munro was already afflicted. Hang on! Rab could be off work one time and Melvin could come over to Farmbank with his wages. He would meet Catriona. Now, given the type of person Catriona is, and given the type of person Melvin is – what would happen? And how would Catriona's mother react?

While I'm building all this up, while all these characters are generating emotions (writing is an emotional job because writers deal in nothing but emotions – human emotion, starting action and reaction, which creates the story), don't forget that I'm still me. I'm still that person who is obsessed with feelings of insecurity, unworthiness and a terrible need to be loved and wanted for herself. I'm writing from this obsession.

Before I know where I am, without conscious thought, I feel that Catriona is dreaming of one day being safe and secure in a home of her own. If Melvin is therefore a widower and has one of these Dessie Street flats . . .

Because I've made Catriona timid and lacking in self-confidence, I make Melvin the opposite – an aggressive, conceited bully. Plenty of conflict (and therefore a strong story) should come from that situation when those two characters come together. One must push characters to their limits to get the most drama and feeling so I made Melvin not only a widower with a son, but a widower who is obsessed with the perfection of his first wife.

Now, I personally knew the emotion of this situation. The agony Catriona felt was my agony. But so was Rab's. And so was Jimmy's and so was Sarah's. In all of these characters I was revealing a kind of nakedness to the world.

I learned a great deal from the writing of *The Breadmakers*. I learned, as I say, how to do research and that one must always check and double-check and triple-check if possible. Never just accept what one person tells you. It may be *his* truth but it might not be the whole truth. For instance, apart from the invaluable facts about the art of baking and what machinery was used, and so on, I got the picture of that old master baker as a benevolent patriarch, loved and respected by all his employees. It really gave me a lovely, cosy picture and I was all set to reflect it in my book ... And yet? Instinct, sheer intuition, made me insist that I visit the bakehouse later, on my own, without the old gentleman, to put my questions again to the other bakers.

The master baker said there was no need. He had told me everything. There was nothing else anyone could tell me. Still I persisted, making the excuse that I needed to see the bakehouse during the night (the old master baker only worked days now) to soak up the different atmosphere. Eventually I got my way and one night when everyone else was sleeping, I set off through the dark streets to the bakehouse. That journey was invaluable, for a start. Glasgow is a different world in the middle of the night. The bakehouse was a different place in the

79

middle of the night. The bakers were different people in the middle of the night. While I sat eating hot, freshly baked rolls oozing with butter and drinking tea from a mug, I listened sympathetically to them. I discovered that far from being a benevolent old gentleman, their boss, as far as they were concerned, was not only a mean, foul-mouthed old tyrant, but a right randy old bugger as well.

When I was working on *The Breadmakers* I was on my own and playing everything by ear. Well, I say on my own but in actual fact I soon found the Mitchell Reference Library in Glasgow and the librarians there, especially those in the Glasgow Room, of invaluable assistance to me. The man who at the time was in charge of the Glasgow Room was called Joe Fisher. He and his wife are now two of my dearest friends and are regular visitors to my home. But often Joe still teases me about the years I used to come into the Mitchell seeking answers to my many research queries.

'I used to hide when I saw you coming,' he tells me.

No question or problem I presented to Joe or any librarian ever proved too difficult to crack, no piece of information too elusive to track down. I don't mean that libraries do your research for you. You've no right to expect that. Nine times out of ten, however, they can produce a book or books or old newspapers or manuscripts which you can search through and find a treasure trove of helpful material you never dreamed existed. And, as I keep repeating, one thing leads to another.

14

Novel writing is about more than research, however. It's about honesty and trying to understand the root of feelings and the motivation for action. I had felt dominated by my mother and, more times than I cared to remember, deeply unhappy in the family situation.

As I left my childhood and went into my teens and young womanhood, I began to dream of escape, of another happier life, and the only way I could imagine ever achieving this would be if I got married. This, I began to realise, was where I was getting Catriona's motivation from. I, and now Catriona, had been dreaming of a magical prince coming to the rescue – falling madly in love with me and magically whisking me off.

After that, all I could think of was me in a house and choosing everything necessary for it, everything that I would like. Not what my mother would want me to like or do, but just some place where I could be myself and suit myself. I used to sit around my mother's house daydreaming about this imaginary home of my own. I imagined everything down to the very last teaspoon and of course that's what Catriona does too in *The Breadmakers*.

In those days, it was unheard of for a young woman to leave home and find a house of her own, or any kind of accommodation on her own or to share with other young people as they do nowadays. That just was not done. I did at one point try to get away by other means. That, I remember, came about when I saw an advert in a paper that some big firm in England needed people for their office and their factory floor – a nut, bolt and screw manufacturer, of all things – and apparently they needed to recruit people from Scotland for their pay office. It said in the paper that interviews would be held in one of the hotels in town at such and such a time.

Secretly, and with much fear and trepidation, I set off for the hotel. I wasn't afraid or apprehensive about the interview, it was the fear of what my mother would say or do if she found out. I had the interview, I got a job in the pay office and it was arranged that I would travel down to Birmingham in a few days time, all expenses paid of course, otherwise I wouldn't have been able to go.

There was a terrible carry-on when my mother did find out. How could I be so wickedly selfish? God would punish me, I was assured. She seemed genuinely upset. For years we had been almost like Siamese twins. Everywhere my mother went, I had to go along too.

I remember one time going over to a friend of my mother's – it was the Mrs Kirby who used to be a next-door neighbour but Mrs Kirby had now moved a couple of streets away. We were going there and I was just seething inside with the injustice of it all, of always having to accompany my mother everywhere like this instead of having a life of my own.

It's all very well for someone else who has had a good, secure, happy background in which they've grown in self-confidence during the years – it's all very well for them to say to me at that point, 'Why don't you just leave?' But I couldn't, I didn't know how to at that moment. But I did have my wee burst of rebellion, saying to my mother as we walked towards Mrs Kirby's house, 'This is terrible the way you're being so possessive with me. I can't do a thing on my own. I can't have a life of my own. You're always dragging me around everywhere with you.'

To my horror, instead of my mother fighting back as she would have done to my father, she just turned a white, brokenhearted face towards me for a moment and I could see the tears welling up in her eyes before she glanced away again. Not only had she never thought of herself as possessive in the way that I was accusing her, but she hadn't realised there was anything wrong about it. I had come to the conclusion that my mother thought of offspring as her own flesh and blood and genuinely and in every way, therefore, belonging to her. That was just a fact of life and for me to try to break away was terribly hurtful to her. She couldn't understand it, and it was more than flesh could bear, especially after all she'd had to suffer with my father.

She did have quite a lot to put up with from him by this time because he was now drinking quite heavily. It was difficult, given their relationship, to unravel it and decide who was to blame for what. They were just so different from each other and so bad for each other, although I believe that underneath all the conflict and misunderstandings, they always loved each other, or at least I'm certain my father always loved my mother.

Visiting friends, and especially her dear friend Mrs Kirby, was the form of escape that my mother took. She would sit in Mrs Kirby's comfortable cosy wee house, bask in the happy atmosphere of Mrs Kirby's successful marriage and play the piano for them, give them a wee song, enjoy the cup of tea and bite of supper that Mrs Kirby would produce. My mother would revel in all this before having to go back to the cheerless place that she shared with my father and myself.

I suppose Audley's escape was with his girlfriend. He had known her since school days and now, after work, he and Margaret (Margaret was her name too) were never apart. He was either along at her house or she was in our house, but locked away with him in his bedroom – something that my mother would never have allowed me to do once I had a boyfriend. Even before Audley's early marriage to Margaret, he had withdrawn as much as he could from the unhappy atmosphere of the house and created a private world inhabited only by himself and his sweetheart.

Thinking of our very frequent trips over to Mrs Kirby's house reminds me of one occasion that indicates this kind of possessiveness that my mother had in connection with me – not recognising me as a separate person with feelings of my own. I really don't know yet what to make of this, to be honest. Anyway, we had gone to Mrs Kirby's, and Mrs Kirby's father-in-law stayed with her at this point and he had become ill, just old age I think more than anything. He was in bed in the bedroom off the living room and at one point in the evening, Mrs Kirby came through in some distress and said, 'Oh, that's him messed his bed again!' He had lost control of his bowels. My mother said, 'Oh, don't worry, Margaret's a nurse. She'll clean him up.'

Now, I was just a teenager at the time and I was training to be a nursery nurse in a day nursery. I was finding it difficult enough to deal with babies and young children, and healthy ones at that, and always under the supervision of senior nurses. I had no experience at all of dealing with adults in any situation, and especially not with a man. But my mother said to me, 'Away you go and see to old Mr Kirby.' And then she just turned back to Mrs Kirby and they started chatting away about something else altogether.

I went through to the bedroom and the blankets were still pulled back as Mrs Kirby must have left them. Here was this old man in his nightshirt, lying in a pool of faeces, and when he saw me he tried to pull down the front of his shirt to hide his genitals. It was about as bad and painful to the old man as it was to me. I felt a bit of me died every time something like that happened to me. Somehow, I managed to get the dirty sheets away and clean the old man, then make up the bed again with clean sheets.

But as I say, looking back on it now, I think – as I do about many situations involving my mother and myself – how could she do that? What was she thinking of? Probably she was just trying to please her friend. This is a characteristic most women have, of trying to please people. But my mother certainly didn't seem to be thinking of me or paying the slightest attention to me at the time. Even when I announced I had a new job and was going to Birmingham, she just brushed the news aside at first as stupid nonsense. When she saw my train ticket and I began to pack a case, she said not to be ridiculous, I would never be able to work in an office or survive away from home. I was a wicked girl worrying and upsetting her like this and eventually she took to her bed and lay with her face to the wall in a generally helpless and miserable condition.

I felt terrible but, if nothing else, I had a core of stubbornness about me, a determination, which of course stood me in good stead later when I was trying to get novels published. And so, despite all the terrible upset and warnings about how God was going to punish me for doing this to my mother after all she'd done for me, and the raging of my father against me too, I stuck to my guns. My father was always totally loyal to my mother in any confrontations with anyone else.

When the time came for me to leave, everyone shut themselves away from me and ignored me. As far as I can remember, no one even said goodbye. I was absolutely terrified. I knew really nothing about life outside my mother and father's home. Of course I'd gone out to work but, in a way, the nursery was part of a dream world – in comparison with the real and far more intense world that I shared with my mother. I felt as I did when I used to go to school, wondering and worrying about whether my mother would be there when I got home, everything else just skimmed over the surface of my consciousness. The total and deep obsession I had was, and always had been, contained within the four walls of my parents' house.

I'd never looked after myself before. If there was any problem at work or anywhere else and my mother heard about it, before I had a chance to do anything – even if I'd been able to do anything – she would barge into the place (much to my embarrassment) and speak up for me. Sometimes I felt my mother thrived on conflict, at least on the kind of conflict in which she could be victorious and on the side of what she believed to be right and justice.

After I left home to go down to Birmingham, she befriended an orphan girl and when the girl had to go to apply for a job in domestic service somewhere, my mother went along with her. Apparently they were shown into this big house and the mistress of the house was lounging in bed with a breakfast tray which had been brought to her by a maid. She indicated with a flip of her hand that my mother and the girl were to stand at the foot of the bed. The woman proceeded to give the girl the third degree, asking her about everything imaginable. This went on for some time, and eventually the woman gave a dismissive flap of her hand and said, 'I will let you know of my decision in due course.'

My mother, however, stood her ground and said, 'First of all, I'd like to ask *you* a few questions.' Needless to say, in the end the girl didn't get the job. They were practically flung out of the house, in fact, but my mother comforted the girl by telling her she was better off without that job and my mother would soon find her another, better, job.

My mother, it always seemed to me, had nerve enough for anything. She would have marched into a lion's den as long as she had somebody with her. My mother, poor soul, was one of the kind of people that couldn't bear to be alone and as far as she was concerned, she was as good as alone living with a man like my father.

I understand now how she must have felt when I left to work not only in another town, but in another country. It has to be remembered that there wasn't the amount of travel in those days that there is now. My grandmother had never been out of Scotland. She had only been out of the wee market town in which she was born when the whole family went on holiday once a year. The holiday consisted of one day in Portobello, a small seaside area on the outskirts of Edinburgh. My mother was a married woman before she set foot outside Scotland and that was to some sort of railway convalescent home in the north of England. Birmingham must have seemed to her a very long way away. It did to me too.

Someone must have met me at the station or we must have gone down in a party of people, because I would never have managed on my own. I'm sure I would have got lost or, as my mother put forward as a much more likely possibility, kidnapped and whipped off to some foreign country as part of the white slave trade.

The firm found lodgings for their new Scots employees and I landed up in a very respectable-looking tree-lined street and was allocated to either a villa or a semi-villa (I can't remember which). It was surrounded by tall trees. It was a bigger house than I had ever set foot in in my life – indeed probably a bigger house than I'd ever seen in my life. I was quite overawed and of course very shy but I soon discovered that house was shared by two families.

When I say that my school days and my working life up to that point seemed like a dream, well this part of my life could be more accurately described as a nightmare. The work in the pay office was all right. I soon picked up how to do the job and I think I did it quite efficiently but, strangely enough, my life took on the same sort of pattern as it had always done before.

Work in the office skimmed the surface of my attention and the intense reality was now centred in that gloomy big house, now my home situation. One of the couples, if I remember correctly, had two children. The other had three but the three children belonged to the sister of one of the women. I don't know if their mother had died, or what, but her sister had now taken over these three children. So there were five children altogether. The faces of these poor wee children haunt me to this day. They were cruelly treated in every way, including physically, and yet the two couples were to all outward appearances great Christians. The minister even used to visit them every week and one of the women would sit like an angel playing hymns on the piano and the five children, perfectly clean and beautifully dressed, would stand all around the piano singing the hymns. The minister was obviously full of admiration.

We all used to go to church on Sunday, the two couples marching on in front and the children and myself following behind. And yet, in the privacy of that house, there was another world that was anything but Christian. One day when I came home from work, one of the men was sitting with a long stick and he was wrapping a length of rubber or leather around the end of it and sticking it to the wood. He told me that this was to beat one of the wee girls and the extra material round the stick would prevent the bruising becoming too obvious. One of the women said – laughingly told me, as if it was something to be proud of – that before the woman from social services came to make her regular visit to the three children that I presumed were orphans, the woman used to put the one that had had a beating in the bath and try to bathe away the bruises, so the social worker wouldn't see them.

The two couples slept in the one room and, although I didn't know of such a thing at the time, looking back I suppose the men were wife-swapping.

There was an atmosphere when the children came in from school, or at weekends – any time the children were in the house. You could almost cut the atmosphere of fear and tension. You could see it in their faces. Even simple actions took on an aura of fear, tension and apprehension.

I have a memory of us sitting at the table in the kitchen. It was a table with a bench seat on either side. I had my tea with the children when I got home from the office and they came home from school. I remember one of the women coming to sweep the floor after our meal but while we were still at the table, and she gave the command, 'Feet up!' All the children, and believe it or not, I too, put our feet up so that she could sweep under the table. She took her time so that we were all acutely strained and tense, trying to keep our feet poised in mid-air until she was finished.

Now, you might find all this hard to believe and wonder why I didn't immediately leave. But think of a four-year-old – would you tell her to make a decision or expect her to know where to report this behaviour or walk out and know where to go and what to do? No, you wouldn't. Well, I believe now, my emotional age was about four years.

Eventually, I was in such a state that I had to get away but apart from anything else, I hadn't my fare home. I plucked up enough courage to speak to the boss in the office, who was a very nice woman. I told her a whole lot of lies about my mother being ill and needing me home for a couple of weeks. I was too afraid to say anything about the awful people in the house while I was still living under their roof. Of course my mother had been writing to me telling me she wasn't well and about all sorts of problems at home and this had been worrying me.

I remember the woman asking me if I was sure I was coming back, because they obviously didn't want to waste their money on my fare after such a short time. I assured her I would be back. In actual fact, all I wanted was to be as far away from Birmingham as possible. At last I convinced her and she gave me a railway ticket for Glasgow.

I was only too glad now to get back to my mother and father's tenement house. The first thing I did when I got there was to sit down with pen and paper and write to the firm and tell them the truth about why I left. The fact was that I couldn't stand the knowledge of how these children were ill-treated and I went into some detail of what I had found out. I never heard any more from that firm but I can only hope and pray that they showed my letter to the authorities and something was done to help the children as a result.

Through going back in my mind and remembering these things, and experiencing again the emotion caused by them, I was able now to understand Catriona's emotions and motivations better. Now I could identify with her, believe in her, and make her seem a real human being.

But what about the other characters, particularly the male characters? How was I going to plug them into the electricity of life and make them totally believable?

15

Alexander Cordell had told me to be honest and I had come to the decision that it was emotional honesty that I should aim for more than anything else.

At the time of writing *The Breadmakers*, I was married to my second husband. He was a widower with a young son. I had had a baby myself by this time – a son by my first husband. He was a sailor and I'd known him for a very short time when he proposed marriage to me. I had immediately said yes. He was a tall, good-looking young man. We were very young. I suppose I imagined I was in love with him. In no time we got married.

I remember I had the most awful job to scrape up the money for a wedding outfit, which I got at one of the sales. It was a brown costume – not very glamorous, and he was in his sailor's uniform. We were married in the vestry of the local church and afterwards had the usual supper of steak pie and peas, and Scotch trifle, in the Co-op hall. We went to a local hotel for one night. I think he was going back to sea next day or just shortly afterwards. I remember saying I wanted tea and biscuits or something to eat when it was time to go to bed. But it was only a delaying tactic because all the silly dreams I'd had about escaping and freedom and having a home of my own suddenly dissolved in the face of stark reality.

Here I was married to a man I hardly knew and in a strange place and not at all sure of what was going to happen to me. I remember him saying, 'Tea and something to eat? We've not long had our supper.' However, he did send for the porter or whoever was on duty and I got my tea and biscuits and took as long as possible over the drinking of the tea and eating of those biscuits.

In the wedding night scene in *The Breadmakers*, Catriona employs similar delaying tactics – or at least her delaying tactics are motivated by the same emotion but the scene centres on her insistence on having a hot water bottle. Any time I read that scene, if I'm asked to give a reading anywhere, I must confess I have to laugh. It seems funny to me when I read it and it does make other people laugh too. But in fact the origins of that situation were anything but funny.

Melvin in *The Breadmakers* was not in any way modelled on my first husband. I must confess, though in many ways, he did resemble my second husband.

16

Maybe my first marriage would have stood a chance had he not been away so much at sea. Because he was away so much, I remained tied very firmly to my mother's apron strings, even though I was living in another flat at the other end of town, a furnished flat belonging to my mother-in-law. She had given us the temporary use of it, which was very kind of her. However, nothing was to my taste. Everything was the reflection of someone else, just as in my mother's house there was nothing that really belonged to me or reflected my personality.

It was a big flat in an old tenement building and it wasn't at all like our building where my parents' flat was. My mother's house was in a Corporation housing scheme which was comparatively modern, and my mother had cheery neighbours and friends all around her that I knew too of course. But this place had, I remember, a dark, cat-smelling close and the flat was on the third floor, I think. As I walked upstairs, I would hear through the shadows behind some of the doors strange music, Eastern music. I suppose looking back now there must have been Asian families there but I don't remember ever seeing anybody except a couple of elderly Glasgow ladies who lived downstairs and the only time I saw them was after I had my baby. He cried and cried and cried and I just didn't know what to do with him and I was in such a state eventually that I went downstairs and knocked on the first door I came to. One of these women opened the door. I was in tears by this time – crying along with the baby. I sobbed out, 'I can't get my baby to stop crying.' The woman took the baby from me and turned away into the house, nursing him. I don't remember what, if anything, was said or what happened after that. In fact, I had quite a time of it with Kenneth crying, but I discovered eventually that he was just hungry. At that point I'd been feeding him with half-cream milk on instruction from the doctor. Eventually I discovered he should have been on full-cream milk and I filled him up with a spoonful of some malty looking stuff as well. After that he started to thrive, stopped crying so much and was a really happy baby.

One of the other memories I have of that flat was when I gave birth to my son. Babies were more often born at home in those days, and not so many people gave birth in hospital. I remember when I went into labour my mother was there and she sat by my bed and every time I took a contraction, she looked as if she was in agony as well – screwing up her face and clutching her hands together, and generally in a terribly tense state. Maybe that proves that she did care about me. Or perhaps she was just remembering the pain she had when she bore her children.

The nurse told her to go home. A gas and air machine was brought to the flat. The doctor arrived and it was discovered that the gas and air machine didn't work. As a result I had a pretty rough and painful time of it. Of course, as soon as I saw my wee boy, it was all worth it. I often say now that he was the best thing that I ever created. My mother adored him and was terribly proud of him. Just days after he was born, I was still in bed with his cot beside me. My mother invited a whole crowd of her friends to come and see the baby and I remember how smoke-filled the room was. Nearly every one of the women was smoking cigarettes. I was worried about the baby – they were all bending over him and admiring him and this cigarette smoke was swirling around him. Also I'd been trying to breast-feed the baby at first but I was having trouble with it. I don't know why but, maybe because of tension, the milk in my breasts had gone hard and lumpy and the baby was having difficulty suckling. Maybe it was because I wasn't putting him to the breast properly, I don't know.

Anyway, there was this problem and one of the people in the room at the time happened to be a cousin of mine. She was a nice kindly person but a bit eccentric. She was also a nurse. I don't know if my mother asked her or if she volunteered, but the next thing was she had clambered up on the bed on top of me and had opened my nightie and was pressing into my breast trying to break up these hard lumps. It was absolute agony! I was moaning and groaning and eventually one of my mother's friends, who must have been more sensible than the others (including my mother), said, 'Maybe we ought to leave.'

My mother cheerfully said, 'Not at all. I'm just going to make a cup of tea.' So nobody left and I had this dreadful ordeal for the rest of the evening.

When I look back at that scene now, it's not myself I worry or bother about, it's the effect that that cigarette smoke might have had on my son. Of course no one knew at the time how harmful cigarettes could be, but nevertheless it seems an awful thing to have happened. Even not knowing how harmful cigarettes were, I'm sure I worried at the time about the atmosphere in that room and the effect it might have on a newborn baby. When Ken was still a baby, that marriage broke up and I went back to my mother and father's house. My mother, and my father too, both adored the baby and took every opportunity to play with him and hug and love him. This was another source of worry to me because, as I mentioned earlier, my father was drinking quite a lot now and he would come in, not staggering or aggressive, but instead of his usual dignified appearance, he would be just stupid-looking, with a kind of gormless grin on his face. He would nurse the baby and try to feed him chips from his pie supper and I was worried this would give the baby indigestion, which it usually did of course. Then I would be up half the night with him crying.

My mother had this obsession with keeping the baby warm. She would insist on piling on cardigans and leggings and hats while he was in his pram indoors, or eventually in the cot that she had for him and kept in the sitting room in front of the gas fire.

I didn't just accept all this lying down, of course. I said to my mother that the baby wouldn't know the good of the clothes when I took him out into the fresh air and the poor wee soul was sweating. You could see it by his bright pink face. I would take the blankets and hat off him but then she would just put them back on. She ignored me as if I didn't exist.

On one occasion, the baby was lying in his cot wrapped up like this. She'd put the gas fire on and the cot was actually right up against the fire. When I had been out of the room, the fire had gone out for the want of a penny in the meter. Someone had then put a penny in the meter and when I went through to check on the baby, the first thing I smelled was gas and I heard the hiss of the gas coming out of the fire. I rushed over, grabbed wee Kenneth out of the cot and rushed to the front door with him so he would get air. My mother was furious when she saw me, came up to me, grabbed the baby from me and dandled him back through to the living room, chatting away to him quite happily.

When I staggered after her because my legs felt like jelly and tried to tell her what had happened, she ignored me and said, 'You'll give the wee soul his death of cold, standing out there with him.'

I used this experience and especially the strong emotions I felt against my mother in a scene from my novel *Daughters and Mothers*. In the scene, Amelia was afraid that she was going to commit murder. She wanted to kill her mother. I knew exactly how she felt.

17

While I was going through this experience in real life, quite a long time before I came to writing that book, *Daughters and Mothers*, when I was actually experiencing that situation, I think it must have been one of the worst in my life. At one point, I had taken the flu or the cold or something, and my mother sent for the doctor. Normally, when that happened – if a doctor had come to see me – my mother would have dominated the scene. She would have chatted away to the doctor, made him laugh, made him a cup of tea, given him some of her home-made scones. If I got any attention, it would have been a bit of a miracle – and you couldn't blame the doctor. On this occasion, fortunately, my mother happened to be along at the shops when the doctor arrived so that I was alone with him. Before my mother returned I managed to blurt out, 'Doctor, I feel I'm going to kill my mother. I'm afraid I'm going to kill my mother.'

To my surprise, the doctor never batted an eyelid, never looked surprised – I suppose doctors are used to all sorts of things and able to take anything in their stride. Anyway, he just asked me if I'd like to see a psychiatrist in the hospital. In those days, to see a psychiatrist was a shameful thing, especially in a working-class area like the one I lived in. However, so desperate was I, so afraid that I might actually do my mother some harm, that I said yes. He told me that an appointment would be arranged for me to go as an outpatient to Stobhill Hospital.

When my mother arrived back, I didn't tell her what I'd said to the doctor but just said the doctor had arranged for me to see a psychiatrist in Stobhill Hospital. My mother, to use an expression she used often, was 'black affronted'. She was ashamed, upset – the likes of this shocking, shameful event had never happened in her family or even my father's family. I was warned not to dare tell anybody.

Anyway, I eventually attended Stobhill Hospital and was closeted in a room with this psychiatrist. I remember him – a very fair-haired man, he was, and I suppose quite a young man. He subtly got me started talking and as I had become a smoker myself by now, I remember smoking all my cigarettes and all his cigarettes as well. I wept as different incidents in my childhood and other more recent ones spilled out. All of them were connected with my mother and our relationship. I wasn't telling them as if anything was my mother's fault. Quite the contrary, it had never occurred to me that anything was my mother's fault. Deep down, I always felt there must be something wrong with me.

While I had been talking, the psychiatrist had his head lowered and was taking notes on a notepad. But at one point, to my astonishment, he suddenly looked up and I could see his face was flushed with what I can only suppose was anger, because he burst out, 'Why didn't you smack her across the face?'

I was struck dumb. I looked at him in absolute astonishment because, for the first time in my life, someone had suddenly taken my side, had taken a different view from what even I had been able to take. Here was somebody thinking – could it really be – somebody thinking that I was in the right, that I was the victim here? The moment for me only lasted a few seconds, so deeply ingrained was the opinion I already held of myself and the type of character that had been formed by my upbringing and environment.

After a time, the interview with the psychiatrist finished and he took me along a corridor into another bigger room and he sat down at one end of the room and I was placed at a desk behind which sat another, older psychiatrist. He started repeating the questions that the original man had asked.

I answered again, still tearful and with head lowered, looking and feeling helpless and defeated. All of a sudden, he slipped in a different, unexpected question.

'And so you want to find a job where you can go and be on your own and leave your baby with your mother?' or words to that effect.

I automatically sprang to life. Looking up, I furiously cried out, 'I'm perfectly capable of looking after my own child.'

I remember how the man smiled and said, 'You know, there's absolutely nothing wrong with you that getting away from your mother won't cure.' He said that they would help me in every way that they could. The main thing was that I had to leave home, I had to get a job and it had to be a job in which I could keep the baby with me.

I tried and tried and could have got jobs, but nothing that meant I could keep the baby with me. While I was still searching – and encouraged by the psychiatrist – I found lodgings just a couple of streets away from my mother, which shows that I was really still tied to her. It was with an elderly spinster who had advertised her room for let. Of course it must have seemed awful to my mother, who had offered me her home. I made the excuse to her and to neighbours that there wasn't enough room for the baby at my mother's place, because my brother was still living there. Also I think I said the other lady had a garden so I could put the baby outside in fresh air in his pram.

In fact the other woman's house was far less convenient than my mother's. There were narrow inside stairs that were a terrible hassle to get the pram up and down. The one room had to contain everything I owned for myself and the baby. I tried to pack everything into the pram when I left my mother's but in the end I had to make two or three journeys back and forward.

It turned out that the spinster lady was very set in her ways. She was quite elderly, had never been married and had never had anything to do with children. She was so set in her ways she even liked the soap in a particular position on the sink in the bathroom and in her kitchenette. Everything had to be in the exact same position that she'd always had it. This, needless to say, made great difficulties for me with a baby to bathe and take care of. Also she complained about the baby crying and I didn't know what to do about that except to go out and walk the streets with him, or just sit in that cluttered room nursing him for hours.

Eventually I saw an advert for a job. It was a widower with a young child who needed a housekeeper. I applied and was asked to come for an interview. The address I was given was a shop in a pretty rough area of Glasgow. I made my way there and when I arrived at the shop, which turned out to be little more than a hut, it was shut. I knocked on the door and a very coarse voice bawled out, 'We're shut!' I timidly said, close to the door, that I had come about the housekeeper's job. The door was eventually opened and in this fousty-smelling wee shop, I saw this man about the same height as myself, balding, broken-nosed. He said he was just about to leave to go home and he would take me with him and we could talk there. He took me home in his car – I think that was the first time I'd been in a private car. His home turned out to be what was called a four in the block. It was in fact much the same as the old spinster lady's house. The entry was from the side and there was an inside stair, at the top of which was a small flat consisting of a kitchenette, two bedrooms and a living room and bathroom. He told me to sit down in the living room while he got changed.

He went through to one of the bedrooms, which was off the living room, and came back through stripped to the waist and holding out a clean shirt he was going to put on. In the middle of the living room floor was one of those free-standing round old-fashioned paraffin heaters and he held the shirt over the heater to let the warm air come up the middle of it while he stood chatting to me. While he chatted, he hitched his shoulders and rippled his muscles as I sat transfixed, like somebody hypnotised. Unbeknown to me at this time, Melvin in *The Breadmakers* was being born.

18

I had broken away at last. I was doing my own thing. I had succeeded as far as the psychiatrists were concerned and I was now on my own. Their faith in me seems touching when I think of it now. What did they think I was going to do? Did they think I would suddenly become mature, suddenly become any more capable? Had I lost my sense of guilt and unworthiness? Quite the reverse! In fact, I'd only been there a matter of days – it must have been just before New Year time – and on Hogmanay here I was on my own with this man in this wee house just across the road from the gasworks, in the small living room. His son, who was about four years of age, and my baby were sleeping in the bedroom off the living room.

When the bells rang heralding a new year, my then employer brought out whisky and poured out a generous first drink for us both and we toasted in the New Year. I wasn't used to drink, of course. One drink would have been enough to knock me practically unconscious, but we had hardly finished the first one when he poured me another. The result was I didn't know what was happening and the next thing I remembered was waking up in the bed settee in the living room where he slept – I had been allocated the other bedroom off the tiny hallway at the top of the stairs. But here I was on New Year's Day waking up in this strange bed. I looked around and to my absolute horror, saw I was lying beside this strange man. He looked really old. He was certainly much older than me.

At that moment I wished I was dead. In a minute or two, he wakened up and he was perfectly calm and cheerful. He got up and went to make a cup of tea. While he was in the kitchenette, I fell out of the bed settee, scrambled into my clothes and just in time reached the bathroom, where I was violently sick. But I was more sick in heart than I was in my stomach. Now I had a real load of guilt to weigh me down. To use my mother's parlance, I had sinned. Of course, I daren't let her know what had happened – that was utterly impossible.

So I began living another double life. Inside that house I was in a situation, as far I was concerned, of being like this man's wife. But outside the house, when I went to visit my mother or anywhere else, I had to remember that I was only a housekeeper. I felt that I must get married. Otherwise I was bound straight for Hell. Somehow marrying the man would rectify the sin I had committed. I was in my twenties by this time – twenty-odd going on for twelve!

As soon as my divorce from my first husband came through, I married again. By this time, I'd convinced myself that I was in love, but looking back, I realise that what I felt was a childish eagerness to please and be loved in return, to feel safe and secure.

I did not feel the kind of love that I'd felt for my very first boyfriend. Long ago I had done part-time voluntary work in a Forces canteen. It was at the same time as I worked in the nursery. I met a Canadian sailor who was about six feet four – I still remember his laughing eyes. He was a really nice young man and, although I can't remember it, we must have gone out together. The only memory I have is of sitting on his knee leaning back against his chest and being held, so securely and lovingly. Occasionally we kissed but mostly he just held me like that, in silence. There didn't seem to be any need to say anything.

I think those must have been the most loving, safest and happiest moments of my life, when I was with him, when I was in his arms. I felt as if I'd known him all my life. When I touched him, it felt so familiar, like part of my own flesh. We were like one person. And yet hardly anything had been said between us. Sometimes we were in the company of other friends that I'd had from school. But he seemed so different from my school friends – so tall, so wonderful looking, so mature, although looking back he can hardly have been more than a schoolboy himself. I thought he was so clever too. He was a French Canadian and as well as speaking with a lovely soft Canadian drawl, he could speak fluent French.

Soon he went away to sea and I waited eagerly for his letters, dreaming of course that he would eventually ask me to go to Canada and we'd live there happily ever after. I received a couple of letters which were heavily censored. Then nothing. Weeks passed, then months. I cried myself to sleep every night. I never felt so miserable in my life. I wrote him an angry letter. Nothing worked. I was absolutely bereft. I agonised about him being killed at some dreadful battle at sea. I grieved.

A long, long time afterwards, when I was in my mother's living room looking for something, I was going through one of the sideboard drawers and I found his letters to me. My mother had not only not told me about them, but she'd opened them and carelessly discarded them in the drawer – hadn't even thought it important enough to destroy them. I was brokenhearted. I tried to make contact with him, but by then he was long gone. He'd left the navy and would have started another career in civilian life. My mother would no doubt have believed she was doing the right thing for me. Not only was my first love a man from so far away, but he was a Catholic. She wasn't a bigoted woman but I'd often heard her say, 'Marriage is difficult enough without having to cope with religious differences.'

Now here I was starting another phase of my life, as a married woman for the second time. Again there was no honeymoon and I just more or less continued with my housekeeping duties. Still I had no home that I could call my very own because in fact it was his home, as he never stopped reminding me and everything in it was his. Every halfpenny in the bank was his. Not only that, but all around the small house were photographs of his first wife, who looked a very pretty young woman with long blonde hair.

He never tired of talking about her and even made me read her love letters and visit her grave with him. He was also terribly houseproud. My usual way, my main object, was to try to please and so I scrubbed and polished when in fact I ought to have been paying less attention to the house and giving more time and attention to the two children, my baby and my little stepson. He started calling me Mummy.

That was of course the first word my son Kenneth used so Calvin started copying it. Oh how I wish now that I had not been such a slave to my husband and his house and instead had played with the children more and talked to them more, made them laugh more. I suppose to be fair I did my best in the circumstances but nevertheless what I remember most is the scrubbing, the hoovering and the cleaning. But no matter what I did, no matter how nice a meal I had ready set for my husband on the small table next to the fire where he liked to eat, no matter what I did, he always found fault with something.

I even got to the stage of polishing the bathroom walls, all to no avail. All he did, apart from criticising me, was to speak about his first wife. She'd been an orphan and she only had him, and she'd died of tuberculosis in the very bed we slept in now, that bed settee.

He used to leave for work in the morning and leave the baby Calvin in bed along with her and when he came home, he would attend to the baby and then to her. Then he cleaned the house – although knowing him, he probably saw to the house first. He would get down on his hands and knees and scrub and polish the linoleum as she lay in bed helplessly watching him. She used to say, he told me, that she would do it but of course she wasn't fit to do it and he told her not to worry, he could manage.

I used to wonder why he bothered about housework at all, because it must have made her feel more helpless and guilty. Surely he had a wrong set of priorities. He also told me that he believed that in marriage the couple needed no one else but each other and he had forbidden her to have anything more to do with any of her girlfriends after he married her, until the day before she died. He asked her if she would like to see the girl who had been her best friend. She said yes and so he contacted this girl, who came and spent the last evening with his wife.

A lump comes in my throat even thinking about this now. That poor woman lying every lonely day by herself, unable to attend to her baby or do anything. Lying there slowly dying with nobody except this man coming home in the evening making her feel even worse.

He, in telling me all this, was boasting about how generous, how thoughtful, how sensitive he'd been in allowing her friend to spend his wife's last hours with her. I was so appalled at this, and in such a state of distress, I got it into my head that he had killed her. I knew of course that he hadn't committed murder, but in a subtle way that nobody knew about – not even himself – it seemed to me that he had helped her to give up the ghost. No doubt it was the product of my overstrained and unhappy mind but I couldn't help asking myself why she wasn't in the hospital getting proper attention. Indeed, wasn't the baby in danger of catching this infection as well? Why wasn't he in a day nursery during the day? Why was there no nurse coming in? Why had he isolated her? Was it just to feed his ego – so that he could boast now that he had been the only one to look after her and devote all his energies to her, as well as working to make them a living?

The size of this ego, and his blindness to what I felt, was frightening. I was in such an overworked, overstressed state, I became afraid that one day the very same thing would happen to me. He would destroy me and nobody would know. Everyone would see him as this saintly, hard-working, generous-spirited man who just lived to do everything he possibly could for his wife and family.

He wasn't the only difficulty either because Calvin, poor soul, had had various people looking after him before me and was a very insecure child. There had been one person, I think a relation of some sort, who had looked after him and, when I met her, she told me – with the same sort of insensitivity that my husband seemed to have – what a marvellous time they used to have with Calvin and what good laughs she had with him. For instance, she said, she used to kid him on that she would wait with a can of petrol behind the door and whenever his daddy came home, she would pour it over it him and set him alight. She said it was a great laugh to see Calvin's face.

I was stunned at this. How could anyone do that to a child? It wasn't surprising that Calvin was a neurotic, unstable and insecure child. I expect he was afraid that I would leave him because one of the main things he kept doing was to cling like a vice round my legs. Nothing would persuade him to let go. I couldn't prise his fingers away and, to the insecure kind of person I was, this was panic-making stuff.

I remember eventually, in despair and panic, slapping him off. Then I was terribly upset because I hate violence and have always loved children. I could hardly wait till my husband came home that evening so that I could discuss the problem with him and get his advice. Between us we had to, I felt, do something that would prevent such a situation arising again.

I started telling him about what had happened and I didn't get very far before he suddenly interrupted me and said, 'You dare lift your hand to my boy again, and both you and your baby will be out on the street!'

So instead of any help, support or advice, I got threatened and frightened. I struggled by myself to cope with Calvin, to try to reassure him and to be as loving as possible to him. It wasn't easy because he had all sorts of insecure behaviour. When we were out, I couldn't step on a bus one second before him, I couldn't put him on the bus before me, we had to step on exactly at the same time. Otherwise he would start screaming at the pitch of his voice in absolute terror, in case I left him.

At one point my husband asked my advice. He had got the chance of going into the taxi business which meant giving up his shop. I could see the possibilities in this and his shop hadn't been making very much – it was just a hut in a very tough area. A lot of people were getting credit and not paying him and so on.

He showed a surprising lack of confidence in himself in making this change. I tried to encourage him and eventually he did take the step, which proved very successful because it turned out to be a real money-making business. In no time it was decided we'd move from the wee house beside the gasworks and he asked me to start looking around for another place.

I found a roomy terraced house in a suburb of Glasgow, in quite a nice area. The house was cheap because it was opposite a sawmill, which lowered the value of it. But I suspected the sawmill wouldn't always be there and I was right. And it was a very nice house. My husband borrowed some money from his father and, added to what he had already, he managed to buy the house without a mortgage.

His father had a dairy business in that same area. I think it was before we actually moved, or shortly after, when he announced that his father and young brother were coming to live with us. His brother was unmarried and lived with the father.

There was no discussion about it; this was the first I heard of it. It was a fait accompli. My husband, by way of explanation, said there was no point in having two housekeepers when one would do.

So the old man sacked his housekeeper and he and his younger son moved in with us. The son was in the fire service and worked shifts. He was a very nice man and really no bother. At least he didn't mean to be a bother but because he worked shifts, there was quite a difficulty with meals. All in all, it was a great deal of extra work for me, not so much because of the young man and his shifts, but because the old man wasn't the easiest person to get on with as far as I was concerned.

The young man emigrated to Canada eventually. I often wish he had stayed in Glasgow because he might have been able to keep his father in line. My husband was no help at all. I remember on one occasion the electricity bill had come in and it was lying on the sideboard. When my father-in-law arrived home from work and saw it, he commented about what a hefty bill it was. I agreed. Then he said not to worry, he would pay it. I was so impressed that I said, 'Oh, Pop, that's very kind of you.' I was thinking to myself, 'Oh, he's not such a bad old stick after all.' He put the bill in his pocket and repeated that he would attend to it. Then he came over to me and although I could hardly credit it, he made a pass at me – he tried to grope me. I managed to shrink away from him and cry out, 'What are you doing? Keep your hands off me!'

His face twisted and he sneered at me, 'Oh, are you the old-fashioned type?'

I said, 'It seems I am because I don't want any of that carry-on!'

Then he took the electricity bill out of his pocket and flung it at me saying, 'Well, you can forget that then.'

When my husband came home from work that day, I was still upset and I told him what had happened. He just laughed and said, 'Oh, he's obviously in his second childhood.' And that was that. As far as I knew, he didn't say anything to his father or do anything about it.

I was still, by the way, trying to write during the years that all this had been happening to me, still without any success. Over the years, in fact, this need I had to communicate, this desperation, had become stronger. It was now an obsession.

I was willing to take help and advice from anyone, but up to this point, I hadn't had any. I showed a short story to my husband but his lip curled and he just threw it aside.

I came to the conclusion eventually that my writing was viewed by him as some sort of threat. But it was while we were living in that house in the district called Cardonald that he unexpectedly came up with the suggestion that he would help me to write a book. He would tell me what to put in the evening and the next day I was to write up what he'd said. He would read it over and correct it and make more suggestions, and so it went on.

In my desperation to become a novelist, I gratefully agreed. So it came to pass.

Of course, looking back, I can see this confirmed the terrible feeling that I had acquired from living with my mother that I was a non-person, just a possession. Now I was in much the same situation, if not worse. But as I said, so desperate was I to be a novelist and I suppose to establish some sort of persona for myself, that I accepted the situation of my husband telling me what to write.

I suffered the humiliation of the instructions he gave me about one of the characters in the book who was the housekeeper. He described her as a cripple. The hero in the book was given the job as a writer, or what my husband imagined a writer should be like, smoking a cigarette in a long holder and wearing a velvet smoking jacket, sitting at a beautiful desk looking thoughtful. The hero's first wife in the book had been absolutely angelic and adored him. The poor cripple woman was nothing in comparison with the beautiful wife, but she was pathetically grateful for any attention the hero eventually paid to her.

I felt humiliated as the contents of the story unfolded and showed that my husband was using me to write a eulogy to his first wife. Not only that, he was revealing what his opinion was of me. Apart from all this, it was also jolly hard work trying to write the book. It was hard work on the level of technique but, apart from that, there was the actual time involved, the difficulty of fitting the writing work into all the other work I had in cleaning the house, making all the meals, doing the shopping, the washing, the ironing, looking after the children and looking after my husband and father-in-law.

At the same time my mother was still in the picture. She seemed to hate my husband from the moment she met him and he hated her. She would get on to me about him and when I was with him, he would get on to me about her. She would say how I was allowing him to dominate me and bully me, and he would say the same about my mother. I came to feel like a bone between two fighting dogs.

It may well be that my husband felt under pressure at this stage because, although he had this kind of arrogance that I've mentioned, at the same time I was beginning to discover that he was really not a strong character at all. In many ways I had a stronger character than he had. He never took any initiative at all, including finding the house we were now living in. I wonder about his state of mind at this time because my mother really was putting the pressure on. She kept wanting me to leave him and come back home with her. She kept nagging at me. With one thing and another, I don't know how I survived that period because I was under such stress, such pressure, such tension.

My husband never stopped nagging at me. I tried everything. I tried ignoring him, I tried reasoning with him, I tried to answer back and argue with him – nothing worked. Indeed, if I tried to argue with him or talk back, that made him a hundred times worse. On one occasion, it got too much for me. It sounded as if he was completely insane. He had picked on the fact that I'd been to the doctor with rheumatism in my hip. He started going on like a madman, calling me all kinds of filthy names as if I'd gone to the doctor to reveal myself to him and have an affair with him. I tried to put my hands over my ears and escape his nagging voice but he followed me around the house until I eventually went hysterical and started to scream and scream. My father-in-law was upstairs and he rushed from his room shouting, 'What's happened? What's happened?' That solved the situation temporarily because my husband hastily hushed both his father and me and smoothed the whole situation over.

I remember everything going round in my mind and I got to the point when I just could not cope any more. I couldn't go on. I suddenly said to myself, 'I'll just have to leave everything to God.'

The moment I said that to myself, I had the most exquisite feeling and also, just for a few seconds, it was as if I was suffused in light. I know that no one will believe this. And, of course, I realise that there could be a rational explanation. It could be that I suddenly relaxed so completely that the relaxation caused the exquisite sensation. I don't know. All I know was that, although things didn't change in any way, and my circumstances remained the same, somehow I got through them. I was able to cope a bit better.

19

A deep reservoir of emotion was forming, something that in the years to come I could draw upon, make very good use of in every book that I would write. Characters too were queuing up waiting to be written about or at least used as models or triggers for characters in my novels.

The first book, that I consciously drew on some of the material from real life for was *The Breadmakers*. I worried – and I realised this was where the courage that Alexander Cordell had spoken of came in – in case my husband or anyone else would recognise themselves in the book or indeed what turned out to be three books, eventually published in one big paperback as *The Breadmakers Saga*.

I came to realise eventually that I had nothing to fear. Using the techniques that I had learned or was learning and putting the characters into a framework of fiction, the only person who claimed to recognise himself was a man whom I hadn't put in any of my books. He claimed to be the handsome, sensitive talented young hero in *The Breadmakers*, a young man who had in fact been based on my brother, Audley. This character in my opinion was nothing like this man in real life and it just reminded me of the quote from Robert Burns:

> Oh wad some pow'r the giftie gie us
> To see oursels as others see us!

I have learned that nobody does see themselves as others see them.

I had meant *The Breadmakers* to cover about eight years or

so in the lives of my characters. That way I'd get the Second World War in. However, once I'd written what I thought was an average book-length manuscript I found only a year had passed. That's why I had to press on and write a second book, *A Baby Might Be Crying.* I wrote it while *The Breadmakers* was bouncing back and forward between Glasgow and London with depressing regularity.

New characters kept popping up with new story lines until I was interweaving so many I had to keep myself surrounded by notebooks in which I kept track of everyone's age, their relationship to each other and where they all were and why. I suppose this is where John Braine's 'full-scale engineering in words' comes in. The age business is especially tricky and complicated. You've got to know all along the line what age every character is and what ages their children are in relation to other children and to fictitious events that are going on and to real-life happenings of the time.

I had to press on and write a third book in which to work everything out to a satisfactory conclusion. I called it *A Sort of Peace* and I wrote it while *The Breadmakers* and *A Baby Might Be Crying* were collecting rejection slips and costing me a fortune in postage.

Mind you, I wept. Oh, how I wept. But it wasn't so much (if at all) over the rejection slips. It was the sheer exhausting hard work of it all. Talk about blood, sweat and tears! *A Baby Might Be Crying* was the killer. I'd given myself two main and serious challenges in this book. First, I'd introduced a new character called Alec Jackson into whose mind I went. Secondly, I brought in the war, part of which is seen through Alec's eyes.

It wasn't the first time I'd gone into a male character's mind, of course. I had done this with Jimmy and Rab in *The Breadmakers.* For a woman writer this is always a difficult and challenging thing to do and I'm not saying I found it easy with the characters in *The Breadmakers.* However, the models that I had used for Rab and Jimmy had been my father and my brother. I had taken certain characteristics that I had observed in them over a long period and from these closely observed characteristics I had created my fictitious male characters.

Alec Jackson was something else. I'd modelled him on a relation as well but this relation was a man I'd only met briefly a few times since my childhood. All I had to go on was a memory of his laughing, sexy eyes and the habit he had of taking a naughty double meaning out of everything anybody said. I had a feeling he was a bit of a rascal but attractive with it. Likeable too. From this vague feeling, I created Alec Jackson and I believe the reason he comes to life more vividly than Rab or Jimmy as a person in his own right is because I remembered my father and brother too well.

Then, as I say, there was the war and Alec had to go to war and I had to be there with him.

And all the time I was realising more and more how I loathed and detested war and the terrible suffering it caused.

Before long, I knew Alec. I knew how he would view the whole business. I simply wrote what Alec saw.

Another character in that book was Sammy, a CO (conscientious objector). Again, I didn't write out of some pre-planned commitment. I didn't create Sammy as my anti-war mouthpiece. Sammy became a CO because of his hatred for his father, who was a military man and a tyrant. I based Sammy's father on my paternal grandfather. Not that my father was ever a CO. In fact he ran away to the army when he was only a young boy. His mother had died when he was twelve and he had been sent to live in the nearby town of Bathgate to live in digs and to work on the railway. I believe it was during that time that he ran away to the army but they sent him back to Bathgate when they discovered he was under age. As far as I could see, his father was a real shocker. With a father like that you had to at least try to escape.

115

Once I had a CO on my hands (I was going into his mind too; I think I must be a masochist), I had to find out all about COs and how they were treated. That certainly gave me more drama and plot material. I had a whole scene at a tribunal, for instance, which was perfectly authentic. I'd interviewed an old Quaker man for information about how Quakers ran mock tribunals to help COs prepare for the real thing. There was also the set-up in the detention unit of Maryhill Barracks which I got from men who'd been imprisoned there. Another scene in that book takes place in the barracks and involves a fight between Sammy and two very tough soldiers. I remember sweating over the writing of this in my efforts to get it realistic. I thought I'd done a pretty good job but – as usual – I decided to check it to make sure. I gave it to one of my sons to read, warning him as I did so, 'Don't be shocked, son. It's rough and there's some bad words in it.'

He read it then fell about laughing, 'Call all that fisticuffs tough? For goodness' sake, Mum. Get the boot in!'

I immediately rewrote the whole scene in an entirely different manner.

Catriona – now married to Melvin – is also in this book and she is involved in the air raids. I drew on my memories of the raids on Glasgow when I was a child and how we all used to troop downstairs every night (we lived in the top flat at the time) and take shelter in Mrs McWhirter's windowless lobby. She was our neighbour who lived in the bottom flat. I remember my mother wasn't very popular on one occasion when she gazed heavenwards in the direction of the German bombers and announced, 'God help them. There's some poor mothers' sons!'

In *A Baby Might Be Crying* everyone takes shelter in the windowless lobby that separated the bakehouse at the back from the shop at the front. In the book something terrible happens and people get killed. In real life the worst that happened in Mrs McWhirter's was when, one night, Mr Kirby, another neighbour, went to the door to peep nervously out, then suddenly staggered back howling among us. We thought a bullet or a piece of flying shrapnel from bombs or anti-aircraft guns had got him but it turned out that the blast had crashed the door shut on his fingers.

By the time I had finished *A Baby Might Be Crying* I had said something important – at least it was important to me – that I had not set out to say at the beginning. It's an odd fact that artists achieve the effect of a message usually only when they don't intend it. Their sermon is most efficacious if they have no notion they are preaching one. They are like the bee who produces wax for her own purposes, unaware that folk will think up different uses for it.

20

You never really know about people though, do you? That's why I say a writer should never make snap judgements, should never take anyone at face value. My father used to glower at my mother and insist he was an atheist. If she put the wireless on at a church service he would switch it off. She would switch it on again. And he would switch it off again. It was one of their battlegrounds. The switch on, switch off usually came at the climax of one of their arguments. My mother's dogmatic illogicality drove him out of his wits.

She was the same with everybody. I remember on one occasion she was arguing with my son Kenneth. She had stated quite categorically that it was violence in books that caused violence in people. Kenneth raised the point about jungle tribes who could be very violent, even cannibalistic, without ever reading any books. Her reply was a triumphant, 'Aye, but the rascals *would* read them if they got the chance!'

My father when alone with me preferred to use the term agnostic to describe himself. Yet often I even wondered about that. He never missed hearing, and watching on television, the Pope giving his yearly message. He seemed to genuinely enjoy and appreciate the occasion, even find comfort in it. I think, too, all the colour and pageantry fired his vivid imagination. I believe my father was a very emotional man – though I don't think he would have liked anyone to say so. He prided himself on being able to keep a cool head in an argument. He used to say to me, 'Never allow an argument to sink to a personal level.'

In his bookcase, as well as his Left Book Club books, there were titles like *How to Argue and Win* and *The Art of Logical Thought*. No doubt they had stood him in good stead in his early days when he'd been the only working-class man on the West Lothian Education Committee but with my mother they were worse than useless. No matter what the topic happened to be and no matter how my father struggled to stick to the point, he was always defeated by my mother's special brand of illogicality.

They would be debating the Spanish Civil War, for instance, and she would say, 'You're a fine one to talk – you that spent three pounds on drink last week. The publican's wife will have a fur coat all right!'

He did worse than take a few drinks. I remember one terrible time my mother had left him for some reason or other. She was always leaving him as a punishment and while she was away she would write in her dashing scribble a long, confusing, unpunctuated letter with a liberal sprinkling of capital letters whenever and wherever it took her fancy, cataloguing his sins and informing him what he must do or must not do in order to get her back.

In reply she would receive a single page of such tiny, neat, beautifully formed words, it was truly a work of art. It took the form of an apology and always ended, 'Yours sincerely, Samuel Thomson'.

'Would you look at that?' my mother used to say, showing me the letter. 'We've been married for donkeys' years and he still puts "Samuel Thomson". Did you ever hear of such an awkward man in all your life? I'll Samuel Thomson him!'

There was usually a present waiting for her when she did return. I remember once a lovely half-set of china that my father had set out ready for her in all its splendour on the living room table.

But the time that sticks in my memory was when my mother returned to find he'd sold her piano. I had been left behind as usual and I was standing in the doorway of the front room when she came in. I must have been quite small because I had no idea what was happening or why. I looked up at my mother and saw her stunned face. Panic smacked across her eyes before she could stiffen against it. It was the first time I'd seen her look vulnerable. It had always seemed to me that she was on the winning side.

I don't know why my father did it. I was too young to know. Maybe he desperately needed the money and had no choice. Maybe there was some reason that he couldn't help. I hope so, because if he did it simply as a means of getting the better of my mother, it was horribly cruel.

But, despite the fact that she reeled under the blow and must have suffered an agony of loss, she was far from allowing anyone to get the better of her. She played a neighbour's piano instead. She had a defiant ripple at everyone's piano. Until eventually, God alone knows how, she got another piano herself.

She refused to be defeated by anything. It seemed to me, on the contrary, that her motto was 'Attack is the best form of defence'. I remember one occasion when she'd found a letter in my father's suit pocket. I don't know what it said exactly but I gathered it was from a woman and she was thanking my father for helping her out by giving her a sum of money. My mother had immediately gone for Mrs Kirby and, with Mrs Kirby by her side, she had marched down to where the woman lived. I don't know what happened because I wasn't there, but I can imagine my mother facing up to this woman and not only getting to the root of the situation but also telling her exactly what she thought of her.

There is a chapter in *Daughters and Mothers* which illustrates how I used this incident. Victoria is based on my mother and Mrs McDade on Mrs Kirby (although Mrs Kirby neither looked nor behaved in real life like Mrs McDade). In the real incident, my mother and Mrs Kirby went down to the busy area of Springburn to confront some unknown woman in one of the tenements there. In the fictional version, Victoria and Mrs McDade get lost out in the country searching for Matthew, Victoria's husband (based on my father), and his secretary, Caroline Ridgeway.

The chapter is very funny. The real incident was desperately serious.

21

After having finished *The Breadmakers* and *A Baby Might Be Crying*, I started on the third book of the trilogy. In this book, *A Sort of Peace*, I explored a mother-in-law/daughter-in-law relationship. The book covered the last part of the war and the post-war period.

I dealt with the real emotion but not the real people. Julie, a shopgirl from the Gorbals and her RAF husband, had nothing in common with my sister-in-law, who belonged to Balornock, and my brother, who would never have been physically fit for any kind of military service. Nobody could be less like my mother than Mrs Muriel Vincent, Julie's mother-in-law in the book.

By the time I came to that third book I had already set characters in the north side of Glasgow and in the south of the city but I hadn't yet characterised the east and the west side. I say characterised because I was in fact trying to capture the character of Glasgow as well as its people. So, I thought to myself – this time I must set one of my main characters in the east side and another main character in the west end.

I started wandering about the west end. At that time I knew nothing about that part of the city. In my wanderings I happened across a lovely leafy crescent that looked down on to the back of the Botanic Gardens. This was the very place, I decided. Before long, as I strolled back and forth along the crescent, I had made up my mind that Catriona and Melvin would move here too. (In the last book they had been made homeless.) I set them in one of the terrace houses at one end.

There were red sandstone flats at the other end and my new west-end characters could live there.

I was just trying to make up my mind about these new characters and visualise them when out of one of the red sandstone buildings emerged a petite genteel lady. 'Are you lost or something?' she enquired. I hadn't realised how odd I must have looked walking from one end of the crescent to the other and back again about a hundred and one times.

I explained that I was a writer and I had decided that one of my characters should live in one of these flats and although I couldn't know what the flats were like inside, I had to at least familiarise myself with the outside of the place, I had to know what someone living here would know about the surroundings. She was entranced. But of course I must know all about the *inside* of the flats as well. All I needed to do was follow her upstairs and wander about inside her flat. What's more, she would make me a cup of tea while I was doing it. Glasgow people really are exceptionally kind.

It was such a help to me to get the proper layout and the feel of that house and to have the lovely green view from the window pointed out to me. It also helped in other ways to meet this dear wee lady because she triggered off a picture of petite and ladylike Mrs Muriel Vincent in my head.

If Mrs Muriel Vincent had to live in the west end, however, that meant young Julie had to come from the east end. Next day I began exploring around the maze of tenements that made up Bridgeton, Calton and the Gorbals. They were knocking the Gorbals down and it occurred to me that it might be a good idea to make a human as well as geographical record of the old place before everyone and everything disappeared. So the Gorbals it was!

When I eventually finished writing that book and therefore the trilogy of books, can you imagine how I felt? It seemed incredible to me at the time that I'd actually managed to overcome all the problems the writing of such a long work entailed. I had a wonderful sense of achievement (and relief). But most important of all was the thrill of having made a whole new world and peopled it with characters of my own creation.

This thrill, this glorious sense of achievement, was worth every tear shed during the writing, every headache, even every disappointment afterwards. (Now I had three books bouncing back and forwards between Glasgow and London.) There's something else too, something almost mystical. I used to listen to lectures by published novelists and they'd tell how one of the characters in their books 'took off on her own' or 'acquired a life of his own' or 'took over and became a person in his or her own right – quite apart from me, the author'.

What airy-fairy nonsense is this, I used to ask myself. Who are they trying to kid?

Yet, believe it or not, by the time I'd finished *The Breadmakers* trilogy – indeed by the time I'd finished the first book of the trilogy – I knew what these authors meant. They had been telling the exact truth.

When I started writing *The Breadmakers* I had no jotter written up for Sarah and when she first appeared in the book I meant her to be no more than the wife of one of the bakers – a very minor character. I intended Catriona to be the one the readers identified with and had most sympathy for. Despite my intention, however, Sarah began to take over. That to me seemed strange enough but what I found quite frightening, almost creepy, was when at one point I was sitting at my desk writing and suddenly, unbidden, out of a blank mind – or was it out of my subconscious? – I heard Sarah say something that was perfectly in character with her but something that was quite alien to me. And I saw her. She shuffled across my mind's eye as clear . . . as clear . . . I cannot tell you. My stomach flips nervously over even yet.

One reviewer said of *The Breadmakers*:

Although the plot holds our interest all the way, the characters reveal the real talent of this author. She cares passionately for people. And it shows. Her portrait of Sarah, the poor, pain-ridden housewife who isn't responsible for her actions is one of the best things in the book.

22

Looking back at it now, I realise that as well as part of me being in Catriona, there was part of me in Sarah as well.

At one point all three books came back to me at once from different publishers. I then made one big parcel of the three of them and posted it to a publisher I hadn't yet tried.

They kept the trilogy for nine months. During that time I kept my hand in by writing another novel. It was called *The Prisoner* and was set in wealthy Bearsden. Or at least mostly set in Bearsden. Three of the characters lived in working-class Maryhill. In quite a few ways this book was different from my *Breadmakers* trilogy. In the first place, it is comparatively short and it hasn't any humour – or very little compared with my other books. Somehow I just couldn't see the main character Celia's predicament as a bundle of laughs, no matter what way I looked at it.

In retrospect, the problems that arose while I was writing that book are hilarious. But, believe me, they were absolutely ghastly at the time and did nothing to enhance my social standing and personality rating in douce and respectable Bearsden. I recall one terrible mix-up when I had to prepare and deliver a speech to a very posh and dignified dinner gathering which included the Lord Provost, local school teachers and other professional people including a couple of ministers of religion.

Now, for anyone who hasn't read *The Prisoner*, it's about a very frustrated woman who discovers that she is married to a homosexual. As a result, she thinks about nothing but sex all the time. And the thing is, as I've said before, a writer has to get under the skin of her characters and really feel as they feel. Well, I wasn't aware of it at the time but when I started to read my speech I soon realised to my horror that I was even beginning to tell dirty jokes! I floundered on, desperately trying to censor myself as I went along. But, at one never-to-be-forgotten moment, I found myself staring eyeball to eyeball with a man of the cloth and out of my mouth were coming the awful words, 'Did you hear about the minister who discovered that one of his flock was a prostitute? He was terribly shocked and upset about this and the very next day he sought out the fallen sheep and said to her, "Oh, daughter, I prayed for you last night." And she said, "Och, you didn't need to do that. I'm on the phone."'

Nobody laughed. Except the Lord Provost, who was immediately silenced by his wife. I was glad when I finished that book. It took a lot out of me.

It took a lot out of me in more ways than one. While I had been writing that book, I was doing a lot of work to the house that we had acquired in Bearsden. I had sold the terraced house in Cardonald by this time and we had moved to this very roomy house in the main street in what was called the village part of Bearsden. Most of the houses in Bearsden were big villas but this was a row of terraced houses in the centre of the area, near some very nice shops. The house had lain empty for eighteen months and the only reason I can think of for that – because it was a perfectly sound building with lovely high-ceilinged rooms and a beautiful hall – was that an elderly person had lived in it before and had never decorated it. The walls were all dark brown embossed paper and there was dark brown linoleum on the floors. The woodwork was all dark as well. The people who had come to look at it before couldn't have had enough imagination to see the potential in that house and what could be made of it.

We got it for a bargain price again, just like the last house, and in due course we managed to sell it (or rather, I did) for a whopping great profit – yet again. Not that I received a penny of it. As usual, the money all went into my husband's bank account. While we were living in the house, we painted it up – white woodwork, pale walls, beautiful tiled hallway, royal blue carpet going up the stairs. It ended up a very nice house indeed.

Alas, I still didn't feel I really belonged. My husband continued to remind me that everything was his, although in fact by this time I was earning some money with short stories. But my money all went into the house and to help with the housekeeping.

Then there was my father-in-law, whom I now had to nurse because he was in dementia and I think must have had Alzheimer's disease. It was a long time, however, before I could get a doctor in for him because neither he nor my husband would admit there was anything wrong. During the day when my husband was in, the old man for the most part seemed quite all right. It was only in the evening that everything went wrong and my husband was out driving his taxi, of course. The old man would start loudly speaking or arguing with somebody in his room and I would discover it was someone who was long dead. Or he would almost set the place on fire dropping lighted papers on his carpet. Or he would waken me in the middle of the night and chastise me for not giving him his tea. Although he'd had his meal, I'd to go and make him another meal for the sake of peace, and he'd eat it in the middle of the night. Or he would disappear and when I went to check on him, he wouldn't be there. I'd search the whole house and if I didn't find him, I knew he must have got out and I'd run outside and quite often I'd find him wandering about dressed in nothing but his pyjama trousers.

The lack of sleep and the stress and strain of all this began to get me down, not just emotionally but physically. My periods got heavier and heavier and eventually just didn't stop. I became physically very weak and anaemic as a result. Helped by the money I was making with my short stories, I managed to get a daily help, or rather a two mornings a week help. She did the hoovering and washed the kitchen and scullery floors.

It was very fortunate that she happened to be in the house one day when I was up on a ladder painting the kitchen ceiling, with gloss paint, of all things, so it was terribly difficult to do. My husband was nagging away about something else that I hadn't done properly, and suddenly, I took a heart attack. I managed to get down off the ladder – I was gasping for breath and, I remember it still, had a terrible tingling, swelling feeling in both my arms and pain across my chest. The home help managed to get me on to the settee and opened up my clothing at my neck. My husband was just looking at me, not doing anything. He just never seemed to have any initiative at all, and it was the home help who said, 'Mr Davis, go and phone the doctor.'

He went to the phone and I heard him say to the doctor that I had rheumatism in my chest. I of course knew it was nothing of the sort. When the doctor arrived – within minutes – he gave me tablets to melt under my tongue and when I was calmed down, I was told to rest and do nothing for a few weeks. Tests were done, and eventually the doctor told me that the tests had shown there was no disease connected with my heart, which was a great relief. He said that it was just the heart muscle and he suspected it was stress which had caused something to go wrong with it.

A temporary bed was made for me in the downstairs dining room and I remember my mother coming to look after me and the house, and my brother also came to see me. My poor brother, pacing round my bed, kept saying, 'Now just keep calm, Margaret. Don't get excited.' Little did we know at the time that his excitement was a sign of his much more serious heart condition.

My mother was in her element, looking after everything, and I remember her insistence that I ate something. I said, 'Don't put a lot of butter on my bread, please, because I can't face anything greasy like that at the moment.' I knew only too well the slap-dash way that she piled butter on everything. As usual she ignored me and came happily through with a tray with tea and cake and bread, and everything spread at least an inch thick with butter.

The butter didn't upset me as much as the fact that as usual she didn't pay any attention to what I had said.

Eventually I got up and life went on as before. I was back to the work routines, which included nursing my father-in-law. My husband by this time was hardly ever in the house. When he wasn't out working – and he did work quite long hours – he was away with his male friends. My husband had bought a speedboat and had it up at Loch Lomond. Several friends often went with him to mess about on this boat. Soon one man in particular was never out of our house. I gathered he was unhappy in his own home. I remember one of the other men had remarked that this man's father was 'a right bastard'. I couldn't help feeling sorry for him as a result. I understood only too well what it meant and how it felt to come from an unhappy background.

At the same time, I resented him. It seemed to me that my husband thought more of him than he did of me. I tried not to show my resentment. The writer in me – which I confess can be a real nuisance at times, both to myself and to others – kept thinking about my husband's motivation. He couldn't cope with how, no matter how much he made a fool of it and denigrated it, no matter what difficulties he put in my way, no matter how much work and how many responsibilities I had, I kept on writing. Even if it meant getting up at the crack of dawn or stealing an hour when his father was dozing during the day and the children were at school, I kept on with my writing. It was something obsessive in me that my husband couldn't get the better of. He couldn't understand it and I think in some way he felt belittled by it.

He had just married the wrong woman and I had just married the wrong man. With a sinking heart, I remembered the disastrous coupling of my mother and my father.

23

One day, my husband brought another man home. He had been a passenger in his taxi and, I was told, was a psychiatrist. He had come up from England to spend some time working in a clinic in Glasgow. He was looking for a hotel or digs to stay in. My husband had volunteered our house and so in this man came as a lodger. Needless to say, there was no question of any consultation with me. This man was the double of Peter Lorre. Younger readers will possibly not have heard of Peter Lorre, but he was an old-time actor, a small, rotund, menacing-looking character with thick pebble glasses and a very foreign accent. This man was exactly like that. I don't know if he was Austrian or German, but he had a very thick accent.

While this newcomer was upstairs unpacking his case in our spare bedroom, I said to my husband, 'How do you think I'm going to manage? I've got the two boys, a big house like this, and your father. (Not to mention a dog, a cat and two rabbits.) I've had a heart attack – I'm still not well. What on earth have you brought a lodger into the house for?'

My husband said, 'I thought that would keep you happy because he's a psychiatrist and you're interested in all that kind of stuff.' It was enough to put me off men for life. I was so harassed and overpowered by it all – my husband, and his male friend who was in the house so often he was practically living with us as well. There was his father, even my two sons and now this other man. All uncaring males. Not that there was anything wrong with my sons, and hopefully they were enjoying happy lives, because Bearsden was a good place to live as far as children were concerned. There were fields nearby to play in, trees to climb and so on. But once this doctor (if he was a doctor) got settled in the house, even for the children that must have seemed a far from happy situation.

He literally took over the whole place and the whole family. My husband was out most of the time either working or away at Loch Lomond with his friends. Under the guise of helping and doing good, this man started telling me and the boys and my old father-in-law what to do – even what we should be eating. Next thing he was in the kitchen making foreign dishes and handing out vitamin tablets to me. Although all this was most unwelcome, I gave him the benefit of the doubt in thinking that he meant well.

But then when we were sitting alone in the sitting room in the evening, he began making passes at me. He kept trying to persuade me to run away with him. I was physically, emotionally, spiritually – in every way – unable to cope with this extra pressure and complication in my life. Looking back, it really is a mystery to me how I survived it all. All I could keep saying was that I was married. His retort was that I didn't have a marriage and that my husband was a homosexual.

This was too much to bear. I refused to listen to anything about my husband and the man became more and more persistent. I was afraid to tell my husband what he'd said but I did plead with him that I wasn't fit to cope with so many people in the house, even with the home help coming in a couple of times a week.

His answer to that came, believe it or not, in the form of a young orphan girl who also came to stay in the house. Yet another extra person, but she was supposed to help me. Where she came from I have no recollection but probably from some place to which my husband had taken a fare and had got to know the people there. She seemed quite a nice girl but she was not long with us when the doctor said to me that he'd seen my husband coming out of her bedroom in the middle of the night.

I didn't know what to do – I was in a state of collapse by this time. This man was constantly feeding me venom of one kind or another. Eventually the girl left and I broke down in tears and told my husband exactly what had been going on, what this man had been saying about him. It so happened that my weekly home help was in that morning and the lodger from hell was there too. My husband normally never took any initiative and to outsiders he was always very meek and mild, pleasant-spoken and kindly.

On this occasion, when I told him what this man had said about him – not only was he a homosexual but he was having an affair with the young girl – he raced into the sitting room where the man was, got hold of him and bawled at him what a bloody liar he was. The man shouted back and before I knew it, I was being pulled between the two of them. The man was pulling at me, saying I would be better to come away with him, and my husband was pulling me back, telling me to get away from the liar and madman. It was absolutely dreadful!

Eventually I escaped from them both and ran out the back door. There was a lane at the back and a garage at the end of the lane owned by people who lived at the end of the terrace. They had a big yard that had a caravan in it. I rushed into the showroom place where the woman who owned it was and just babbled out something like, 'Oh, hide me, please hide me!'

She was taken aback – probably it was the talk of Bearsden afterwards – but she hustled me into the caravan. The curtains were all shut and she locked me in and I sat there in the dark of the van, trembling and cowering and shaking like a leaf. I was in a state of terror. Eventually the home help came for me and when the garage lady opened the door, the home help assisted me out. With her arm around me, she helped me back along the lane. She said, 'Don't worry, it's all right now.'

Then she said, 'I've never in my life come across such an absolutely wicked man!'

I said, 'I know, it's dreadful and I'm married to him.'

She said, 'No, I mean the other one!'

However, when I got back to the house, the lodger had gone. My husband had physically flung him out of the house. By this time, I was like a punch-drunk boxer. I was hardly capable of thinking.

An incident with my son, Kenneth, around this time still haunts me. The Bearsden area was still strange to him. He got lost and I searched and searched for him. Eventually I had to stop because there was the evening meal to make and everyone else to attend to. The state I was in meant that I was only capable of getting through one minute or one hour at a time. One job, one task at a time. After attending to the meal, I would phone the police, I told myself. I was in the middle of dishing up the food and I suppose I looked quite calm, when wee Kenneth stomped in through the back door, through the kitchen and into the front sitting room. As soon as I finished serving everybody, I went through to the room. I found him sitting staring ahead, white-faced. Even as a very young child, he was always so capable and courageous. He didn't cry or complain or anything. I suppose – or I hope – that I was loving and comforting to him then but I have often felt guilty since about the distress and fear he must have suffered, wandering about a strange place in the dark not knowing where his home or his family were.

Then to come in and see everything going on just as normal as if nobody cared about him must have been terrible. Of course, the truth was I cared about him more than anything else in the world and still do.

There were other examples of this characteristic of my son. I remember once I was in the sitting room and I heard him as if he was speaking to himself. I looked out and there he was stamping up the stairs saying firmly to himself, 'I am *not* afraid of ghosts. I am *not* afraid of ghosts.' I discovered that my stepson Calvin was in the habit of hiding in different places and jumping out on Kenneth. One of his favourite hiding places was the bathroom cupboard. When Kenneth went up in the dark to the bathroom, Calvin would suddenly jump out on him. He must also have been telling him that there were ghosts in the place. Kenneth never came to tell me about this – I found out by other means. He didn't tell me about what happened in the bathroom. He just faced it on his own and tried to overcome his fears. I really admired him for that and there have been so many other occasions where he has shown the characteristics that I wish I had myself. I suppose he must have inherited them from his natural father. Either that or he is just his own self and always has been.

I doubt, even if he had told me of his fears and problems at the time, that I would have been able to be of much use to him. I was so overwhelmed. Even just with cooking and shopping.

As well as my old father-in-law, and the lodger from hell while he was there, and my husband, and the two children, there was my husband's special friend who was so often sitting at the family meal table as well. He was a quiet, shy, well-behaved young man, much younger than my husband, and no trouble at all.

Nevertheless there came a time when I couldn't take any more.

24

Once that psychiatrist – if he was a psychiatrist, I sometimes wonder what he was – had left, things didn't improve. At one point I packed a bag and some boxes, and the boys and I carried what we could, and we left the house. I took my stepson with me because I felt I couldn't subject him to the kind of insecurities I'd suffered when my mother left me. We stood along at the bus stop waiting for a bus to take us into town, where we would get another bus to go to my parents' house – the only place I could go. There were no refuges at that time. Not that my husband ever hit me or physically abused me, but there are other forms of abuse, even harder to bear and even more destructive of the person.

I remember as we were waiting for a bus, a car drew up and a man offered us a lift. We piled in to the car and the man must have suspected that I was leaving my husband because as we were driving into town he said to me, 'Are you sure you know what you're doing? Are you not making a mistake?'

I hardly knew what I was doing but I just had to get away. Eventually I arrived at my parents' place and they made us welcome and put us up the best way they could, but of course they were in a much smaller house. The boys managed to get a bed made up for themselves in the bedroom where my mother and father slept, but I had to sleep in the living room on a settee which wasn't long enough for me, and in the morning when my father was getting ready for work, he had to come through for different things. It obviously wasn't a situation that could last for very long, and of course I had no money so I was then totally dependent on my father and mother, and they hadn't any money worth talking about either.

Soon my husband came and took Calvin away. Then when that didn't bring me home, he returned and said that his father was very ill and asking for me. Now, in truth, I didn't go back because of his father, although it appeared that way – I could have seen his father far enough, but I was only too aware that to continue living in the cramped circumstances in my parents' place, and with no money, was quite impossible. That was what forced me to return.

Of course it was to the very same situation as before, even worse in some ways. There was even a frightening, stressful situation outside the house, as well as inside it. By that, I mean everyone in Glasgow was concerned and nervous about a spate of terrible murders that indicated a serial killer was on the loose. People were frightened to go out at night, afraid even to walk through the park during the day. This meant that I couldn't escape outside on my own for a breath of air and a bit of peace. Although – foolishly, as my mother accused – I sometimes did.

My father-in-law was not only suffering from his dementia symptoms as before but he suddenly doubled up in pain. I ignored my husband and phoned for the doctor. I remember I'd phoned for him on a previous occasion, quite a long time before, but, when he arrived, the old man was quite cheerful and sensible so nothing came of that visit.

On this occasion, however, the doctor examined him and a strangulated bowel was suspected. He was whipped off to hospital. I remember as he was being carried out on the stretcher, he looked round at me and said, 'You'll be glad to see the back of me. I've been an awful bother to you.'

I said, 'No, no, Pop, no problem at all and I'll come to see you in hospital. Don't worry, you're going to be all right.'

'No problem at all,' I'd said. My goodness, that was a whopper of a lie if ever there was one. But what was the use of upsetting the old man at such a time? I did go in to see him in hospital but not long after that, he died there.

Before he went into hospital, though, I had phoned the Samaritans – in desperation. I called from a public call box and, just my luck, I ran out of money in the middle of the call but what I did then was to find out where their office was in town and to go there. That's where I met my first Quaker – an old Quaker lady. She was the first one who listened to me with sympathy and understanding, and seemed to care about me. Even when it was only for that short time on that one afternoon, I truly appreciated it and it did help me.

All the time that I was living in Bearsden, I was still keeping my hand in with my writing. There must be a strong bit about me, to have come through all that and still hang on in there, trying to be a successful writer. But I was getting physically weak, even then. I must confess now, as an elderly lady, that although the spirit is still as strong as ever, the old flesh is getting awfully weak.

I went several times to my doctor and he never even bothered examining me. This particular doctor was an elderly man and he had a surgery in his house, which was a big bungalow. Eventually I had gone down, feeling like death, creeping about rather reminiscent of Sarah in *The Breadmakers*, when I come to think of it. I went down to his house where he consulted and he came to the door. I said, 'Oh doctor, I wish you'd give me something. I feel absolutely terrible. Please help me.'

He said, 'Oh yes, I'll do what I can for you. But come back tomorrow, this is my half-day today.'

I was turned away and I think, now that I remember, that it was on the way home from there that I phoned the Samaritans. I also made an appointment to see a gynaecologist. I paid for it with a short story I'd sold. Within seconds of examining me, the gynaecologist said, 'You'll have to go into hospital urgently. You need an operation. You have a tumour.'

I went home and wept as I told my husband. He took me on to his knee in one of the few moments of tenderness I remember of my marriage to him. He said he'd pay for private treatment so that I'd get the operation right away.

I was taken into a private hospital within a couple of days and was given a hysterectomy. The surgeon said afterwards that I'd been in a right mess and they'd had to take away my ovaries and appendix as well. Apparently I looked like death for a time and I remember regaining consciousness and seeing my husband leaning over me. He was waving a bunch of flowers near my face. He had a slightly wild, triumphant look about him and he said, 'I knew you couldn't do this to me.'

I was extremely weak for a while after the operation but something else happened that made me forget about myself and my problems.

25

My dearly loved brother Audley died. It is to his memory that I dedicated *The Breadmakers*. My mother, his young wife and I sat with him hour after hour holding his hand, listening to his terrible breathing as, even in his unconscious state, he fought to cling on to life.

The day before, when I visited him in hospital, I believe he knew not only that he'd taken a relapse but that he was going to die. He looked at me with tragic, fear-filled eyes and said, 'I was up on Christmas Day, Margaret. I was nearly getting out. I sang "Bye Bye Blackbird" at the party.'

I can never hear that song without feeling anguished.

When I was leaving the ward that afternoon (he was alone in a small room and I wish he hadn't been alone), my mother stopped me and said, 'Kiss him.'

And I did.

Then going along the corridor, she told me, 'He's not going to get better.' I still see her face, the depth of her suffering giving it a lovely dignity. Why did I speak harshly to her in reply? I said not to talk nonsense and that Audley was going to be all right. I didn't mean to sound curt or cruel. I suppose it was just that I couldn't bear to face the truth. I didn't have the courage. She had though.

I never saw him conscious again. At evening visiting time his eyes were closed and the room was filled with the nightmare noise of his breathing.

My mother and father are dead now but, much as I loved them, I never wept so brokenheartedly for either of them as I did for my brother. And every night alone in my bed (my husband usually drove his taxi at night), I frantically sobbed out prayers, pleading with God to understand how Audley had been an atheist and to forgive him. (He had asked that there would be no ministers at his funeral.)

I wondered myself why Audley was an atheist. My father was an atheist. Was that the reason? Or was it a kind of survival kit against my mother's overwhelming love for him? She was a strong Christian (the United Free Church). It must have been difficult for a boy to retain his masculinity in his circumstances.

Audley daren't give up or give in. Maybe that's why when he was in hospital with that last illness he told his wife not to let my mother in to see him. Eventually, of course, she had to get in when his condition worsened. I think I understand how he felt about my mother. I know he loved her. But love can make you so vulnerable, can't it? He was only trying to be brave.

He was so clever and talented. He had to leave school early because of the rheumatic fever but he had educated himself. And of course he taught himself to play the piano. (That's why I had Jimmy in *The Breadmakers* play the piano.)

Oh, how I do remember him with his dark curly head bent over the keyboard, his pale face tense with concentration as he forced his rheumaticky fingers to move. He used to pencil above each note on a piece of music C, D, E, F or whatever he had discovered it was. Then with excruciating patience and perseverance he'd find the notes on the piano and play them. He'd play the first bar of the music that way, over and over again with desperate loving care until he'd got it perfect. Only then would he move on to the next bar and so on through the whole piece.

When my brother was small no one could have been more loving and patient with him than my father. Audley adored him and, right to the end, no matter what my father did or didn't do, Audley remained hotly loyal to him. That was why it was so tragic that, in latter years, my father acted as if he violently hated Audley. (Not all the time, of course, but violent emotion began to explode to the surface more and more often.)

Who's to blame? Who starts what? And why? I don't know. All I'm sure of is that a novelist should at least try to understand, should try to work out motivation, not blame. I think my father's attitude changed as he became jealous of my brother. I suppose this happens quite often in families – the mother favours the son and showers him with love and attention, perhaps to the neglect of the husband, and, in this particular case with my brother, my mother was so worried about him when he took rheumatic fever. She had to nurse him in the house and the poor boy was in such agonising pain. She did what she could for him and spent every waking moment as far as I can remember caring for him. Because of the intense love my father had for my mother, and the love he had for his son, his feelings became all twisted and mixed up with jealousy.

I never saw my mother shed a tear over Audley's death. But my father became distracted and went around the house whimpering Audley's name. And within a matter of weeks he had collapsed with a heart attack. He survived that first attack and my mother said to him, 'Why should you be alive and my son dead? Why couldn't it have been you?'

She must have been tormented by a terrible burden of bitterness as well as grief. But I can see her yet at the funeral tea held in her front room after everyone had returned from my brother's cremation.

The room was crowded and her handsome, straight-backed figure moved briskly about seeing to everyone's needs. The way she was behaving in her usual cheery hospitable manner, no one could have guessed that the gathering was in any way different from the much-enjoyed parties she was in the habit of giving. She even told some of her funny anecdotes and had everyone laughing.

I think, looking back, the time I'm talking about must surely have been the worst period of my life. And yet I suppose it was as much an apprenticeship for the job of novelist as all the practice in writing I'd done. Everything was torn and anguished and confused. From the time of my brother's death I felt I was watching the destruction of my father. My mother never let him be. Even as she and I sat either side of his hospital bed her bitter tongue continuously cut him to pieces and he, with his temper, never failed to be roused into retaliation. It tortured me to see him, eyes protruding in distress, breathlessly fighting back. I could do nothing to stop it. I tried but only made things worse.

The danger of interfering is that no one knows the whole truth about a relationship, not even one of the family, and the person trying to help only adds more fuel to the fire.

My father was a big powerful man. He survived that heart attack but he was never the same again. By this time, he'd lost his job on the railway. He became terribly anxious about money and the future. He got into panics too easily. Even if he couldn't find his spectacles, he panicked. My mother said it was sheer lack of control like his wicked bad temper.

They fought tooth and nail until the day he died. He had been along the road at the local pub for a drink. When he returned he couldn't find his Post Office savings book, which he thought he'd had in his pocket. He got into one of his panics and I can just imagine how, at the same time, my mother's tongue would be flaying him. He left to go back along the road to look for his savings book. But, for no apparent reason, he returned within a couple of minutes and, as my mother told me later, 'He just stood in the doorway and looked at me. And I said, "Well? What are you standing there for?" Then, without answering, he turned and went away again.'

On reaching the pub he collapsed, blood gushing from his mouth, and he was dead before the ambulance arrived.

Afterwards my mother wept and said to me, 'Oh, the pity of it!'

I never saw her weep again but later when I was in a shop with her helping her to buy clothes for the funeral she suddenly looked at me in anguish and said, 'Was I not nice to him, Margaret?'

What could I say in the circumstances? I immediately reassured her that of course she had been nice to him and he had always thought the world of her. As indeed he had. 'Your mammy's a wonderful woman,' he used to say.

She seemed to be reassured and, in the weeks and months and years that followed, I've listened in absolute astonishment as she's related stories to friends about 'my Sam' and what a wonderful husband he'd been and what a beautiful and happy relationship they'd had.

'Never once did a cross word pass between us,' I've heard her say.

She also used to tell everyone that 'poor Sam' had 'dropped in the street'. Alone with me, however, she'd say, 'Fancy him dying in a pub!' As if, perverse to the last, he'd done it just to spite her.

My father always carried the key of the coal cellar about in his pocket. In their last house there was a coal cellar out on the landing next to the front door. They didn't need it for coal because in that house they had an electric fire but my father used the cellar to experiment with home-made wines. My mother hated 'the demon drink' and so never went near the place.

After my father died, I was given the task of clearing out his things. Eventually I got round to tackling the coal cellar. I unlocked the door. Inside, there was no wine. There were hundreds of bars of soap and quarter-pound packets of Co-op tea and tins of corned beef and mountains of baked beans and packets of my mother's favourite 'pink pudding'.

Here was my father's fearful insecurity, his desperate, secret efforts to provide the necessities of life for my mother and himself in their old age.

My mother never worried about tomorrow.

'Tomorrow will take care of itself,' she used to say. 'God will provide.'

But my father was an atheist.

26

My mother and father were devastated by my brother's death and my mother took a dislike to the house they were living in. It was an unlucky house, she insisted. She came to hate it as if it had killed my brother and no doubt it had. Certainly the dampness in it had caused his original rheumatic fever, although he hadn't slept in that damp room for over a decade.

My father was impatient with my mother's idea about the house. I don't know if he said anything to her but he often said to me that it was a whole lot of nonsense talking about luck or bad luck in connection with a house. She kept saying she wished she could get a house near me in Bearsden.

They didn't have the money to buy a house and so I made an effort, tried my very best in fact, to get them a rented house near me in Bearsden. The last thing on earth I wanted was to have my mother living practically on my doorstep. I knew if that happened, she would just take my life over again and never be out of my house.

I've always had a certain amount of pride and didn't want to go around begging for houses to rent but I did. I went to the bank because there was property above the bank to rent. I sought out people who I'd heard let out property. I pleaded with them, I used all my writing talents to write letters on my parents' behalf but of course there was a limited amount of property to let in a place like Bearsden at the best of times. There were only some flats in the village part, mostly above the shops. My mother, and even my father too, kept visiting me in Bearsden, obviously hoping that I would manage to get them a place. My father adored the boys and was very good with them, and I think he wanted to be near them but, although I really did try my very best and left no stone unturned, I didn't in the end manage to get them a place.

The sad, defeated expression never left my mother's eyes after that, although with her usual courage and spirit she continued with the fight to keep going. Her grief and sadness and bitterness were kept private, except when the bitterness was aimed at my father.

She took in lodgers and for quite a long time she had a part-time job working as a cashier in the restaurant of the La Scala picture house in Sauchiehall Street. There she kept everybody cheery with her chat and her interest in everything and the customers who came in. She used to regularly visit the YWCA in Bath Street, which was quite near the picture house, and she would go in on her way to or from work, or both, and cheer everyone up there and entertain them with her piano playing and singing.

I remember one of the lodgers she had was a waitress. She wasn't a young woman by any means and, being on her feet all day, she used to come in at night really exhausted. On one occasion when I was visiting my mother, this woman came in looking drawn and tired. She mentioned that her feet were killing her and my mother made her sit down, not move until she was given a cup of tea and then as she drank her tea, my mother brought through a basin of hot water, knelt down in front of her and bathed the woman's feet. That was how kind my mother was and what a good friend she was and why she was held in such high regard and genuine affection by everyone who knew her.

I think she had begun to take in lodgers and work in town to keep herself out of that house as much as possible. And when she was in the house she always had to make sure she had company. Many a time, as well as being heavy in heart, I'm sure she must have been tired and footsore herself but she insisted that she enjoyed being out, especially in such a job where she met so many people. My mother had always been a very extrovert person. She blossomed and flourished and was in her element when she had an audience.

27

Glasgow is full of interesting people and one of the most interesting I met was a Miss Reekie, who could speak Urdu and who acted as a kind of liaison for the immigrant community.

Miss Reekie invited me to her flat one Sunday afternoon. What a fascinating afternoon it turned out to be. Her front room was crowded not only with Pakistani men, women and children; a few West Indians and Chinese had come along for good measure. The place was so packed, half of us had to sit on the floor. The talk was so loud and, to a Scotswoman like myself who had never been used to any foreign accent worse than English, it was most terribly confusing. I'm sure my ears must have grown that day, I was straining and stretching them so much. It wouldn't have been so bad if one Chinese man hadn't kept playing the flute.

At one point, I was jammed on a sofa between him and a plump Pakistani lady called Mrs Mogul, who was knitting furiously and talking even more furiously about a journey she and her husband had recently made to England. While in that country she had gone into a shop and the shopkeeper had asked, 'Where do you come from?'

Mrs Mogul had proudly replied, 'I come from Glasgow, Scotland.'

'What?' sneered the shopkeeper. 'That dump!'

'You no' like Scotland?' Mrs Mogul was outraged even by the memory of the occasion. '"I no like England!" I told him!' She flung her knitting down and went, muttering, to help Miss Reekie with the tea.

I was joined by a pretty Pakistani girl called Shafiga. But before we could get talking, Miss Reekie herded a family of five little boys into the room and announced that they were going to give a song. They were lined up and, after a few proddings from Miss Reekie and everyone else who was within prodding distance, they burst into a charming, if somewhat squeaky rendering of 'Jesus loves me, this I know, for the Bible tells me so . . .'

Eventually the Chinese man put down his flute so that he could drink his tea and I got chatting to Shafiga. She invited me to visit her home. As a result, a few days later I was making my way somewhat nervously along one of the poorer streets of the city. It was a dark, winter's night and all I could see around me in the shadows of closes and at street corners were dark-skinned men who were talking in a strange tongue. I was later assured that I was safer in that street among the Pakistani men than among anyone else, anywhere else in Glasgow. Pakistanis have a respect for women, I was told, and for the safeguarding of a woman's good character. My friends told me they had a saying, 'If money is lost, nothing is lost. If health is lost, something is lost. But if character is lost, everything is lost.'

Shafiga's father had been a trained dispenser in Pakistan and had been called 'Hakim' or 'Doctor' and treated with much respect. Over here, however, his qualifications were no use and he was too old to start a new training. Eventually, the only job he could get was as a lamplighter.

'Margaret,' he said to me, 'this is no good for an old man. I have the sore knees with up down, up down so many stairs. My legs they feel they are walking all the way to Pakistan and back!'

I learned so much from these people and I owe them a debt of gratitude. I was jolted into a new awareness and understanding. Things I'd taken for granted, or never thought about, had to be thought about and looked at in a new light. Even small things, like when one of the sisters, Nargus, the youngest, a teenager still at school, told me excitedly that she was wearing new trousers.

'Look, Margaret! New trousers!' she cried, clapping her hands. She was in seventh heaven of rapture and I couldn't see why. They were nice enough trousers but all the same . . .

'Bell bottoms!' she squealed. 'Bell bottoms, Margaret!'

It was only then that it occurred to me why this was such an exciting and unusual event to her. All her life until then she had been forced to wear the tight at the ankle Eastern trousers. Bell bottoms were Western dress. She had made a break with tradition, taken an exciting step into a new world. Suddenly I understood how she felt. I began to understand how these women felt in lots of other ways. Especially the older women. I began to see how frightening and shocking our Western way of life can seem to them. It is part of their religion, for instance, that a woman should be modestly covered from head to toe. When my Pakistani women friends visited me at first they used to hastily cover their heads with their scarves if my husband entered the room. They also rose to give him a seat, which was somewhat off-putting for him. When he offered to give them a lift home they stared at him in nervous silence until I, sensing it wasn't the done thing for them to be alone with a strange man, offered to go too.

The majority of older women in Pakistan were illiterate. Almost all of them, for all their lives before coming here (at least at the time I'm talking about), were hidden by the burkah, a heavy tent-like garment with just a tiny grating-type window for the eyes to peer out. Think yourself into a burkah for a minute. Firstly, nobody can see you. You don't need to have any expression on your face at all. There's no need even to acquire the habit of smiling. Your face will be relaxed and completely untutored in the lively, varied, sophisticated range of expressions that have become second nature to us in the West. Imagine having that protective covering suddenly ripped off, and in a strange land where everyone is a different colour and speaks a different language, and has different customs and philosophies.

The first difficulty I had to struggle with was the language. I became particularly friendly with Parveen, the married daughter, whose husband Ibrahim worked on the buses. Parveen had been taught English at school in Pakistan and she spoke very good English – as did they all, except 'Mummy', who couldn't speak any. Even with Parveen, though, the accent – part Glasgow, part Pakistan – made it very confusing. We had all sorts of misunderstandings and mix-ups. Like when I arrived for a visit and I thought Parveen said, 'Will you have coffee or tea?'

'I'll have tea, thank you!' I promptly replied.

But Parveen had actually said, 'Take off your coat, please.'

I wondered at her surprised and bewildered expression. Then, when the truth dawned on me, I was terribly embarrassed.

'You must think I'm awfully cheeky,' I said, apologising.

'No, no, you are not cheeky,' she hastened to assure me. 'You have tea or coffee or curry or chapattis or anything in our house. You are like family. We have a love with you!'

The really difficult thing to grasp and to practise is not the language, however. It is the switching over to see everything from their viewpoint. The only way I can explain this is to give another example.

While talking to Shafiga I discovered that Muslim parents arrange marriages for both their sons and their daughters and there is no such thing as having boyfriends or girlfriends or courting before marriage. I thought it was the natural thing to do to show sympathy when discussing this with Shafiga.

'That's terrible!' I said indignantly. 'You should be free to choose your own husband. It should be your choice!'

To my surprise, she answered with matching surprise, 'But why? Can it be that I am wiser and know more about these things than my mother and father? No, no, I trust my parents to do what is best for me. They love me, you see.'

'But,' I persisted, 'what if the marriage doesn't work out? What if you are incompatible?'

Shafiga replied, 'Oh, there are very few divorces in our country. Pakistani women are very reasonable. If we do something which does not please our husbands, our husbands only need to tell us – and we change!'

Other Pakistani women joined in our conversation and were curious to know how we in the West met our marriage partners. Do you know, I found that a kind of difficult thing to explain.

'Oh, er . . . at parties, or clubs, or dances, I suppose,' I murmured vaguely.

They were horrified.

'But that is madness!' they cried. 'Marriage is a serious business. It requires much serious thought and discussion and investigation before a partner is chosen – someone with whom you have to share your whole life . . .'

It began to occur to me that I must not take it for granted that they would approach any subject with the same premise as me. As a result, I had to keep readjusting my thought processes, keep starting from scratch, so to speak. I had to practise thinking like someone who had been conditioned by totally different habits and standards and ideas from me.

However, despite the difference in language, customs and outlook, I found my new friends basically the same as me and any other folk I knew, and I believe that as long as we can cling to this idea of our common humanity or, as the Quakers say, 'that of God (or good) in every man', then difficulties can and will be overcome. (As my mother used to say, 'Where there's a will, there's a way.')

Unfortunately one of the things everyone seems to have in common – and my Pakistani friends were no exception – is the

As a wee girl, c. 1932

On a pony ride while on holiday, c. 1935

With other Red Cross Voluntary Aid Detachment nurses
(back row, third from right) at an English naval camp, c. 1946

My family attending a cousin's wedding, c. 1938. In the back row, from the far right to left, are my father, Samuel, my mother, Christina, me and my brother, Audley

Here I am – on the left – as a teenager, enjoying skating with a friend at a local ice rink, c. 1934

As a young woman, c. 1960

Pausing for inspiration, c. 1964

Doing a bookshop signing, c. 1966

Correcting proofs, c. 1972

A proud mum – Baby Kenneth was born in 1953

Looking relaxed and happy at a party with other writers, c. 1980. I am in the front row, fourth from the left. In the back row, second from the left, is the writer and journalist Cliff Hanley and seated at the far right is Lavinia Derwent of *Tammie Trout* fame

With fellow writers (back row, far right), including Alanna Knight
(in front of me) and 'Mr Glasgow' Jack House (next to me) and,
seated far left, the historical novelist, Nigel Tranter, c. 1982

My first grandson, Martin, lends a tentative hand with his granny's latest novel, c. 1986

Speaking at a writers' conference, c. 1996

With my arm round Norman Wisdom's shoulder at a writers'
conference at Swanwick, Derbyshire, c. 1996. Both Norman
and I were invited speakers at the conference

With four writer friends at a writers' conference, c. 1996

With three friends at a charity dinner, c. 1998

With two dogs in the grounds of Traquair
House, the home of my good friend Flora
Crichton, c. 1999

Glasgow's Provost Alex Mosson presenting me with a Lord Provost Award at the City Chambers, in 2002. My award was for 'bringing Glasgow's vibrant history to life in [my] novels'.

Here, I am being given a beautiful bouquet in recognition for the help I have given to aspiring writers

Proudly displaying my Lord Provost Award medal, alongside just a small sample of my many novels

tendency to nurse prejudices against sections of our fellow men and for the same reasons of lack of knowledge and understanding.

White people used to try to tell me that Pakistanis ate dog meat and did other things which didn't do much to encourage me to take them to my heart. But of course I discovered that in fact my friends who were Muslims were very particular about their meat. Like the Jews, they preferred their own butchers where the meat was bled in a special way and prayers were said over it. And they didn't eat pork because they considered it dirty.

They were most particular about personal cleanliness too. In fact, I'd never come across folk who washed so much!

But my Pakistani friends were prejudiced against Hindus and would say to me, 'Never have anything to do with Hindus, Margaret. They are dirty people. They sprinkle cow's urine over everything in their houses. They worship the cow. They are also idolaters.'

I'd never met any Hindus and I made a mental note that I didn't fancy them and would be very wary if I ever came across any. Then, one summer, my husband and I went on a bus tour to Europe. We visited seven or eight different countries and ended up spending a week in the Austrian Tyrol. Now, right away, when our bus party set off I noticed this solitary Indian among us. He looked very shy and miserable hanging back in a corner on his own. Think of how you'd feel yourself if it was the other way around, I told myself. How would you feel alone in India with nothing but coloured folk all around you and all talking away in a strange language? I worried about this Indian feeling lonely and not understanding what the courier was saying and maybe forgetting his passport and not getting the kind of food his religion obliged him to eat and not being able to explain to anybody. Soon I overcame my own shyness and went over to him and asked him if he was getting the right food and if he was all right. I invited him to join our crowd of friends. This, I learned, was his first trip out of India. He'd flown over for a short visit to his sister and brother-in-law in London and was now doing this coach tour to see Europe.

It turned out he was a Hindu. That shook me a little. Then I thought – well, we all have our funny little ways if you really get down to thinking about it. And what was a little cow's urine between friends? (Actually he was most fastidious. He was always disappearing away to his room to have a shower and change his clothes.)

We became good friends together, Sharad Babu and the rest of our little group. Many a good laugh we enjoyed together and what great talks we had. Sharad willingly answered all my questions about his customs and religion. I was most touched by his feelings about his wedding night. He said it was the most beautiful and treasured moment of his life when he first saw his wife's face. (It was an arranged marriage and he'd never seen her before the wedding.) But there happened to be two single beds in the room in which they spent their wedding night and he was too desperately shy at first to approach his wife's bed. He had a gift to give her as was the custom, a beautiful ring. But he took it to bed with him and just lay there on his own, fearfully anxious and wondering what to do.

Then, just as he was plucking up courage to leave his bed and go across to his wife, he discovered he couldn't find the ring and had to rummage frantically in the bed to try and recover it. Eventually he found his gift offering and the courage.

Later, when he got to know his wife better, he asked her how she had felt that night as they lay in separate beds and she replied, 'Very worried.' (Well, you can imagine!)

As I said, he answered all my questions about his religion too and soon I could see, from his point of view, Hinduism was just as reasonable a thing to believe in as the Muslim religion, or the Jewish, or the Catholic, or the Protestant . . .

In fact, Sharad Babu just about converted us all, if not by his religion, at least by his charm and his enthusiastic and unsophisticated affection for us.

Although again, of course, there was the odd little language difficulty. Like when he told the young honeymoon couple of the party, Ruth and Ralph, that he fancied them. He just meant that he liked them very much. Then, of his room-mate Frank (who was a big Welshman), Sharad waxed wildly enthusiastic and said, 'Frank is so sweet and innocent. I love him!'

Actually there was an odd kind of naivety about big Frank and we knew what Sharad meant. Sharad, in fact, became so overcome with emotion about us all that he'd hug Frank and my husband and George – another member of our group of friends. Or he'd slap their knees or link arms with them and me while sitting on the long back seat of the coach as we careered along singing happily through all the different countries.

I'll never forget these spontaneous demonstrations of loving friendship between ordinary human beings who had somehow got over the barriers of different customs, religion and tradition and met on equal and trusting terms in the middle. It was yet another of the many lessons I learned in becoming a successful novelist.

28

So now I had five novels on my hands, counting the awful one my husband had helped me with. (Actually I had *ten* novels because I'd already written another five, remember!)

I decided to post away *The Prisoner*. I wanted to have another read of *The Breadmakers* trilogy to see if there was anything I could do to improve it. But where to send the new novel? It sounds crazy but I decided to send *The Prisoner* to the publisher who had just rejected my trilogy and for no other reason than that the firm's name began with 'A' and I thought I might as well work my way through the alphabet. Within a week I had a letter saying they had decided to publish my work and it was now only a matter of deciding which novel to do first and would I please send back the trilogy! After all these years – a lifetime – I get four novels accepted at once. It was an incredible thing to happen to any writer.

I was still living in Bearsden at the time and I had been along at the shops and was feeling none too sprightly as I slowly returned to the house trundling my shopping trolley behind me. I opened the front door and when I got into the hall I saw this letter lying on the floor. Picking it up I noticed it had a London postmark and I thought it would be an acknowledgement of delivery of my new book. When I opened it and saw what it said, I actually leapt and danced around the hall like a dervish. Then I went dashing and shouting through the house but no one was in to share my good news. (This was the news, by the way, that was later met with complete silence by a gathering of relations.)

In double-quick time I had the trilogy winging its way back to London and it was decided to bring out *The Breadmakers* first. Before it came into print, however, the publisher was on the telephone to me with a few queries. Up to that point I'd always taken it for granted that, although I was a Scotswoman, I spoke and wrote plain English. Not so! Before the publisher was finished asking what this word meant or that expression meant, I felt an absolute foreigner. I discovered that without even realising it I had used many Scotticisms. I complied with the 'translation' that the publisher suggested. All the same, I felt and still feel that the meaning was clear enough in the context in each passage. And, after all, I as a reader have to cope with books by English authors and Welsh authors and American authors.

But I had discovered by this time that some London publishers and agents had a 'thing' about Scotland and the Scots. I began to think that they didn't like us very much up here. They seemed to have the idea (in those far-off days at least) that we were a crowd of ignorant savages running about with razors hidden in our kilts!

Anyway, my books have all sold well. *The Breadmakers* trilogy, now known as *The Breadmakers Saga*, has been reprinted several times and is still selling a lifetime later. It has also been adapted for the stage. There is always, I'm told, a huge waiting list for my books in all the libraries, and they are up there just a whisker behind Harry Potter. (In the libraries, at least. I wish they sold as well in the bookshops and made me an income even a fraction of what J. K. Rowling earns.) *A Baby Might Be Crying* was once voted Top Book in one English library. At one time, another of my books, *Rag Woman, Rich Woman*, was the most borrowed book in the Strathclyde Library Service. Both *The Breadmakers* and *Rag Woman, Rich Woman* were successfully adapted for the stage and *The Breadmakers* won a Festival prize for drama. And I was eventually asked for a follow-up to *The Breadmakers Saga*.

But before all of this, lots of other exciting things happened. When *The Breadmakers* was first published, I went to London and was wined and dined and interviewed by the press.

The paddle-steamer *Caledonia* had been featured in my book and it was discovered that this old ship was no longer plying up and down the Clyde but was sitting on the Thames in London. A party was arranged on board to which journalists and magazine editors and paperback publishers came. It all seemed like a dream.

Even after I came home, lots of journalists kept arriving on my doorstep to interview me. One interesting point that emerged from all these interviews (which were not about the book, by the way, but about me) was that, on the whole, the articles seemed to be more like reflections of the journalists' characters than mine. It seemed to me that I was reading about a different person in each newspaper feature.

Some journalists had stronger personalities than others and I remember one lady, who was also taping our interview for radio, briefing me beforehand with, 'Now, I'll say . . . and then you'll say . . . And then I'll ask . . . and then you'll reply . . . and then I'll say . . . and then you'll say . . .'

Although I tried to remember and struggled to give all the answers she clearly thought I ought to give, my heart wasn't in it. The interview was a bit of a shambles and as far as I know was never accepted either for print or for radio.

My second book, *A Baby Might Be Crying*, had an even better reception and I was particularly glad about that, not only because it had been such hard work but also because that book meant a lot to me.

The third of the trilogy, *A Sort of Peace*, was hailed as the best of the three. By this time I was receiving letters from ordinary readers telling me they had enjoyed my books. Some also told me their life histories and all their problems. Some people even sent photographs of themselves. I came to the conclusion that there must be a great many lonely and troubled people about.

Hearing from readers and learning how much they appreciated my books made all the hard work worthwhile. Mark Twain said, 'The public is the only critic whose judgement is worth anything at all.' Maybe he's right, I don't know, but it is certainly a great thrill and most heart-warming to hear from readers.

Next, the publisher commissioned me to write a historical novel set in Glasgow. I didn't know anything about historical novels to begin with, of course. I hadn't read a historical novel since I was in my teens and I hadn't a clue how to write one. But I said yes, then worried about it afterwards.

Many years later, another publisher asked me to write a book about a Pakistani family arriving in Glasgow in the early fifties, when Pakistani families were just beginning to come over. I said yes to that publisher too, then worried about it afterwards.

With me moving house and with them moving to England, I'd lost touch with the original Pakistani family I'd known. So now I had to approach local families, explain about the book I'd been commissioned to write, and ask if I could interview them about their experiences. They all agreed and I had invaluable and fascinating help from them, especially the Shafaatulla family, who owned the local grocery shop. As a result, I managed to write a successful book called *In a Strange Land*. Unfortunately, the publisher of *In a Strange Land* was only a library supplier and so the book didn't get into any bookshops, although I think if customers order a copy in a bookshop, they could perhaps get one.

But long before the Pakistani book, when I was commissioned to write my first historical book, there was no one to ask, no one to interview. Also, as well as not knowing anything about historical novels, I knew very little about history. Gradually, however, I became aware of a hazy recollection of having heard something somewhere about Glasgow tobacco lords.

Off I went to the Mitchell Library. 'I'm thinking of writing a book about the Glasgow tobacco lords,' I told the librarians in the special room that housed the Glasgow Collection. 'Could you help me?'

They could.

I began with a few 'character notebooks' of fiction characters as I'd done with *The Breadmakers*. This time I was greatly helped by reading about the actual characters – rich and poor – who lived in and around the city in the eighteenth century.

I discovered, too, the knack of blending into my fiction narrative real-life characters and incidents gleaned from books about old worthies, and newspaper reports of happenings and biographies of men and women of the period. (Journals and diaries are also great sources of material.) I came across some hilarious anecdotes which I incorporated into my story – like the funeral where everyone got so drunk, it wasn't until they reached the graveside that they discovered they'd forgotten the body.

I enjoyed writing my eighteenth-century historical trilogy in the end. Yes, like *The Breadmakers* it turned out to be not one book but three! Before long I found myself enthralled and the more I read, the more I gravitated towards the poorest folk of the time. With them I could best identify. Soon my eighteenth-century characters were as vividly alive to me as anyone in *The Breadmakers* or my contemporary novel, *The Prisoner*, had been. In the end, I not only enjoyed writing that book, I enjoyed the research almost as much. What fun I had reading some of the journals of ladies and gentlemen of the time. From them I picked up the rhythms of the speech and the favourite expressions and words they used. I laughed uproariously as I wrote certain scenes, just as I'd done while writing *The Breadmakers* trilogy. Other scenes made me sob brokenheartedly. I remember the first time I appeared with my face all tear-stained and swollen after writing a scene in *The Breadmakers*. My sons cried out in concern, 'What's wrong, Mum?'

I sobbed in reply, 'Jimmy's just died.'

'Who's Jimmy?' they wanted to know.

I had to explain that he was a character in my book. They groaned and rolled their eyes. It's a terrible trial having a writer as a mum.

In *The Prince and the Tobacco Lords* another character, whom I had only intended to be a very minor person in the book, 'took off'. Old Quin, the beggar, I don't know why, just grew and grew and there was no getting away from him. When he and I had to say goodbye there was a very painful lump in my throat. (Long after the book was finished I'd find myself wondering what happened to Quin.)

The other two books of that trilogy, *Roots of Bondage* and *Scorpion in the Fire*, are set half in Glasgow and half in America. Needless to say, the American research presented difficulties, but I wrote to the Research Librarian at the University of Virginia, who was most helpful. She also put me in touch with an American publisher who specialised in books about the period. As a result I obtained books like *Women's Life and Work in the Southern Colonies* and *Colonists in Bondage* and *The Secret Diary of William Byrd*. This last book was very amusing in places. William Byrd was in the habit of making entries in his diary like, 'I said a short prayer but notwithstanding, I committed uncleanness in bed.'

And, 'I rogered my wife, I neglected to say my prayers but had boiled milk for breakfast.'

And, 'Gave my wife a flourish on the billiard table today.'

The mind boggles!

American friends also helped me by sending research material. For the Glasgow side, it was back to the old Mitchell

Library again. I also had at one point to find out about a poison – belladonna or deadly nightshade. I had to know the effects it had if administered to someone. For this I had to go upstairs to a department of the library that I hadn't used before and in which I was not known. You should have seen the suspicious looks I got when I said I wanted to find out what exactly would happen if I gave someone a dose of deadly nightshade! Actually the symptoms of belladonna poisoning are particularly horrible and when I came to write the scene, I really felt quite ill. I'm being perfectly serious about this. Writers suffer from emotional, physical and mental strains, often with embarrassing and traumatic results.

Nevertheless, my life – at least my working life – had at last taken a turn for the better. So maybe my husband would change too. Maybe he'd even feel proud of my achievement. Not a bit of it! If anything, it strengthened his determination to make it impossible for me to write at all.

29

My mother didn't make it any easier for me to write either.

When I was writing *The Prince and the Tobacco Lords*, I would be sitting in my writing room willing myself backwards in time until at last my mind would start flickering with candlelight. I would hear the clatter of horses' hooves outside. I am Annabella Ramsay in my house in the Trongate. The Trongate is busy with people going to the dancing assembly. I'm ready in my hooped skirt, high wig and face patches. I'm impatiently agitating my fan and wishing that my maid Nancy would come and tell me that my sedan chair is ready.

Papa frowns on such frivolities as dancing assemblies.

'Annabella,' he says. 'I forbid you to go to that den of iniquity!'

I fling myself about. I kick and scream and create such a fuss until he agrees, in case I take a fit or worse. Papa spoils me. He acts fierce. He threatens to order the doctor to give me a good bleeding or the hangman to whip me through the streets. And one day . . .

A bell rings. My hand gropes out for it. Someone says in my ear, 'Is that you, Margaret? I just thought I'd tell you that Sadie dropped in to see me last night. The reason she didn't manage on Monday was because her car broke down.'

Eh? Margaret? Sadie? Who are they? A car? What's this? My mind fumbles and gropes back through the mists of time. Horses' hooves fade away and disappear. So does my beautiful gown, my wig with the strings of lammer beads looped over it.

So does my elegant fan and my jewelled snuff-box. There is no longer any sensation of anything.

The mist clears. I see bookshelves, a filing cabinet, a desk, white paper, a pen in one hand, a telephone in the other. I remember who Sadie is.

'Oh, yes, how is Sadie, Mum? I've never seen her for ages. Oh? Oh. Piles. Oh, dear. Yes. Painful things. Uh-huh. Oh, the poor soul! Oh, fancy! Isn't that terrible? Oh, I know. See doctors! Uh-huh. Oh, isn't that awful . . .'

My mind is now full of Sadie's sufferings and it takes quite a struggle to banish her and her piles from my thoughts. I'm also left with the irritation of my mother's now constant and anxious query of 'Are you all right?' Talk of Sadie was only an excuse. Since the death of my brother and my father, my mother had developed an anxiety complex about me. She also had a terror of being alone.

Of course she had never liked to be on her own. She had always been a very gregarious person. Sometimes, looking back, I think she missed her vocation and should have been an actress. Immediately a visitor arrived or immediately she joined a gathering of people, it was as if she stepped into a spotlight. Her face lit up. Her brown eyes sparkled. She held herself like a queen. She spoke confidently and entertainingly. She told funny anecdotes. She played the piano. She sang songs. If there was a violin or any other instrument in the place she had a go on that too. It wasn't that she was a show-off or in any way boastful. In fact it wasn't until after my mother died that I discovered she was actually qualified to teach music and was an LRAM (Licientiate of the Royal Academy of Music).

I never knew her to have any patience for reading music, far less for carrying it around. If anyone asked her if she could play a particular piece, she'd say, 'Certainly! How does it go?'

The enquirer would find themselves having to try to hum or whistle anything from 'Mares-eat-oats-and-does-eat-oats' to

Beethoven's Fifth. After a few bars my mother would brush them impatiently aside with 'Och, aye!' before plunging from one end of the keyboard to the other in an energetic and impressive flourish. No key was left unused. Then she would give a spirited rendering of whatever piece had been requested.

She enjoyed bursting forth into song as well, some of her favourites being 'Bless This House', 'The Old Rugged Cross', 'If I Can Help Somebody' and 'Abide With Me'.

It never worried her if she forgot the words halfway through. Without as much as a pause for breath she made up words of her own to fit in, and just as smoothly transferred to the right words once they came back to her. It was the same with music. If she went wrong in a piece or forgot the tune, she stamped her foot defiantly down on the loud pedal and flung her fingers about in a crescendo of chords or merry ripples until she remembered the original melody. I used to sit in an agony of suspense waiting for bits of Chrissie Thomson to suddenly break into Robert Burns or Chopin. It was bad enough in the private houses of friends. In front of an audience in a church hall or YWCA meeting or charity concert or at any public gathering, it was absolute torture. Only to me, I hasten to make clear! Everyone else seemed to thoroughly enjoy the performance. My mother was always perfectly convinced they did anyway.

It was just as nerve-racking when she spoke in public. She would never prepare her talk, never give it a thought, never take a note. She would just sail up to the platform and start to speak without turning a hair.

In answer to my queries about what she was going to talk about she'd say, 'Och, I expect I'll tell them one of my wee stories.'

She meant anecdotes from her own life. Or sometimes she'd tell the audience in her own words about a book or story she'd read and enjoyed. The anecdotes were either funny or romantic or both. The stories were invariably sentimental. It always seemed to me incredible – not only that she could rise to any occasion so effortlessly (if a speaker didn't turn up and she happened to be in the audience she never had any hesitation in rising if asked – or even if not asked – and offering to save the day) but that she could talk in such a rosy, romantic vein. The chances were, not half an hour before, she would have been bitterly battling with my father.

For my part, I would be feeling sick and shaken and harrowed. I would be completely worn out with just having listened to the quarrelling. Sometimes I used to become seriously confused as well. It was as if I was not only losing a grip on life around me, but of myself. I used to wonder what was real and who was real. Could the world of conflict inside our house just be a figment of my imagination? Was my mother actually the happy, romantic person I saw when she was in the company of other people?

This kind of experience stood me in good stead when I eventually became a novelist. I never take anyone at their face value now. Nothing surprises me as far as human relationships are concerned. I have a wide-open mind, ready and waiting, and curious, to see what's going on behind the mask, or behind the net curtains. People all put forward a certain image of themselves in normal social contacts. Myself included, no doubt. So often this gives a very mistaken picture of what people or their lives are really like. It's a novelist's job to recognise the difference between what people say – the image they project of themselves – and what they *do* and *are*.

My mother still had a wonderful spirit – in company at least – after my brother died. But her black hair began to go white and thin and her shoulders became more rounded. She hadn't the same, if any, interest in her appearance. She used to like a nice hat and had always been extremely proud of an apple-green straw boater she'd picked up at a jumble sale for sixpence. I remember a red felt one she was rather fond of which blew off one day and went right under the wheels of a bus. After the bus went over it, she picked it up, punched it back into shape and put it on again.

She had always argued with my father (I've heard him cry out 'I can't say black without you saying white!') but now, it seemed to me, a bitterness she could no longer control, an absolute hatred of my father engulfed her, seethed continuously under the surface of her relationship with him. I may be wrong. I hope I'm wrong. After all, how can I, or anyone really, truly know another person, know their emotions, know what *makes* them feel as they do, know the secret struggle they might be having within?

But I sometimes suspected my mother hated my father even to touch her or go near her after my brother died. Yet, she wouldn't allow him to sleep in a separate room, although he kept being wakened during the night, either by my mother getting up to go to the bathroom or to make herself a cup of tea because she couldn't sleep. Then when she did sleep she kept him awake with her snoring. He had his work to go to next day and he was getting quite frantic with fatigue. But she wouldn't let him go. (Not that there was anywhere to go except the living room sofa. They didn't have another bedroom or front room in this house. They didn't even have a bed settee.)

It seemed even then she couldn't bear to be alone.

From the day my father died, two of my cousins who were nurses stayed with her night and day because she refused to spend a moment alone in the house. She would have given the house up the day after the funeral if I hadn't persuaded her to wait for a few months before making any decisions about what she was going to do or where she was going to live. I told her she would be welcome to stay with me until she got over the shock of my father's death and could think about things more calmly and clearly.

That first day when she arrived at my house in Bearsden and ·I took her up to the bedroom I'd made ready for her, she looked around and said wistfully, 'I could stay here for the rest of my life.'

My brain keeps blanking out now. I try to turn my mind's eye inward to examine myself and the events that followed but it's as if there's a wall blotting out memories. I strain against it until my head aches yet nothing comes to me through the blackness except a very few disjointed scenes.

I remember when she first saw the room. I remember the slight relaxing of her muscles. She looked as if she thought she was safe. The room was very small, no more than a narrow boxroom. The bigger room at the back which had been my father-in-law's bed-sitting room was much larger. Since he had died, however, it had been converted into a writing room for me. It now contained office furniture and bookshelves packed with reference books. But I had tried to make the small room as pleasant as possible, with a pretty bedmat and a rug and pictures on the wall and a vase of flowers on the chest of drawers. It was bright and that was what mattered to my mother. She could never at any time stand dark, dull places and she could never bear the colour black. Even at the funerals of my brother and my father she could not bring herself to wear anything black. The room also faced the front and was cheery with the noise of traffic and people. But, most important of all, through the wall in the next room was where I slept.

She must have been in a very bad state of nerves by this time, although she never complained and still in company she was, to all appearances, her normal cheery self. I remember, though, the first morning I went to give her a cup of tea in bed, I couldn't get the bedroom door opened. I couldn't understand it and after calling to her, I heard loud thumping and scraping noises. When my mother eventually opened the door, I discovered that she'd had the chest of drawers jammed up against it to secure it shut. Every night I'd hear her lock herself in and pull the furniture up against the door.

I can only bring to mind two other scenes from the six months during which my mother lived with me. And even those are not too clear. One was when Kenneth was either being mildly disobedient or cheeky to me (it couldn't have been anything serious because Calvin and Kenneth have always been good boys) and my mother started talking to him as she used to talk to me about how God worked in strange and terrible ways.

'One day He'll take your mammy away from you,' she told Kenneth. 'You'll never see her again. Then you'll wish you hadn't spoken to her like that.'

I immediately exploded in her astonished face. I was shivering violently with emotion.

'Don't you dare speak to him like that! Never speak to him like that again, do you hear?'

Hurt and bewilderment replaced her surprise. Tears shimmered in her eyes.

'But I was only sticking up for you,' she said.

I was beyond myself, stuttering with the violence of my emotions, incapable of channelling them into lucid expression.

'You're not going to make him suffer with guilt. You're not going to do to him what you did to me. I won't let you!'

Afterwards I felt more wretched with guilt than I'd ever done in my life. The poor soul had lost her son and her husband. The last thing she needed was me shouting at her as if I hated her. I tried to be extra loving to make up for it and she immediately and gratefully forgave me.

I began to have some inkling of the terrible conflict of emotions she had suffered while living with my father towards the end of his life. I began to be torn with conflicting emotions myself. I struggled frantically to keep them secret from her. The worse I felt inside, the calmer and more loving I forced myself to act.

I can only remember one other scene. It was New Year's Eve. We call it Hogmanay in Scotland and it's the custom to 'stay up for the bells' and to either go out 'first-footing' or welcome any visitors who arrive to 'first-foot' you after midnight. Whisky and wine and cake and shortbread are made ready and the family all wait for the chimes of midnight. Then they all kiss each other and wish each other a Happy New Year.

It's unheard of to go to bed before midnight and not be with your family to bring in the New Year. But I couldn't face it. I just couldn't. Perhaps I was worn out beyond endurance with nursing my father-in-law. I often think that if I hadn't had him – and, after all, he'd been with me all my married life – I would have had enough emotional and physical energy to cope with my mother and look after her for the rest of her life. By this time, you see, she had given up her house. The day she walked out of it to come to me she had said, 'I'll never live here again.' And she was true to her word.

Maybe it was the strain of having to cope with my mother's inability to be left on her own, even for a few minutes in a room, that was too much for me. She followed me about the house during the day. I could no longer go into my writing room. It was even a worry to get to the toilet. If I went shopping she had to hurry and get ready and go out too. At night it was impossible to leave her in the house. She had to either have a friend come and see her or she had to go and visit a friend. And she was getting less and less able to go out. I was glad now of my husband's friends visiting. My mother enjoyed their company. I remember her remarking, 'What nice lads. Especially that quiet, shy soul. But I'll soon bring him out of himself.'

That New Year, the first since my father's death, I just went to bed at the back of eleven, shut my eyes and pulled the bedclothes over my head.

I heard the bells. I heard the clink of glasses. I heard my mother and my husband wishing each other a Happy New Year. Knowing what he thought of my mother, I marvelled at him being able to carry on the charade.

That's all I can remember. But my mother must have known that the situation couldn't continue because it was after that she started talking about going into an old folks' home.

30

I have a tape of my father telling my sons a story when they were small. But I haven't played it since he died. I don't think I could bear it.

I remember the occasion. It was in our house in Cardonald and the boys had a tiny low-ceilinged room upstairs. The idea of the tape-recording was that on the evenings when 'Papa' wasn't there, the boys would still be able to hear him tell one of his stories. I insisted, however, that he shouldn't get them all over-excited or they'd never be able to sleep, so it had not to be one of his hair-raising tales. A storybook called *Timmy Tiptoes* was handed to him with the firm instruction, 'Now, Daddy, none of your carry-on. Read this quietly to them and no nonsense!'

Then I switched on the tape-recorder and left the bedroom. Before I reached the foot of the stairs I heard the children's giggles swirling into hysterical hilarity. I could imagine the funny faces my father would be pulling and the mock seriousness of his rendering of *Timmy Tiptoes*.

Whatever he was doing, it was causing a riot and I marched back upstairs to give him a stern ticking-off. On my return journey to the bedroom, I could hear his conspiratorial giggles and whispers competing with those of the children. He was a natural with youngsters. He seemed to become one of them and was accepted as such. He was adored as one big, crazy, fun person. And not only with his grand-children. Always, but especially in the last house in which he lived, there was a constant stream of small children – some mere toddlers – knocking on the door and asking my mother if Sam was in. Or, because he sometimes took them to the park, they'd ask if Sam was coming out to play. They never called him Mr Thomson or even Uncle Sam – just Sam. Yet he could be such a shy, awkward, often quite embarrassing man with adults.

I have also a tape-recording of my mother's voice. She is singing her favourite songs and accompanying herself on the piano. I don't have the courage to listen to that either. I recorded it while she was in the old folk's home.

She didn't want to go there. Oh, she pretended she did. She fooled us into thinking she did. I think she even fooled herself. She was always such an optimist, you see. And she not only told rose-coloured, happy-ever-after stories, she *believed* them. She seemed as if she was looking forward to the big day, as if she was going on her holidays. She chatted to everyone about the place as if it was a first-class hotel on the Riviera. And everybody was so nice there, she kept repeating. My mother always spoke of everyone as if they wore haloes and had wings under their coats.

The home was a big, old villa in the west end of the city. The furniture in the sitting room was big and old too, but beautifully polished. Everything was spotlessly clean and tidy. The bedrooms were in a modern extension at the back and they were tiny but each resident had his or her own. The sick bay was also in the extension.

My mother kept stressing, and I kept agreeing, that she would be perfectly free to come and go as she liked. I said I would visit her regularly every week and she could come and visit me as often as she liked. After all, it was only about a twenty-minute bus ride away. It seemed a very happy arrangement. It wasn't until the day came for her to leave our house in Bearsden that the truth dawned on me. She was frightened. Never before in my life had I seen my mother look frightened. Even as my brother lay dying she had shown no fear, only tragic resignation. Each time she left my brother's bedside she told me she just said to God, 'Thy will be done.'

But now her eyes were alert with apprehension and despite the proud tilt to her head, a pulse kept fluttering in her neck. My husband and I took her in the taxi. She was unusually silent.

The elderly matron greeted us kindly and showed us to the bedroom allocated to my mother. We deposited my mother's suitcase on the chair beside the bed and then followed matron to the sitting room to be introduced to all the other old ladies and gentlemen.

Introductions over, I kissed my mother and told her she would be all right and not to worry, I'd see her next day. I waved her goodbye from the room doorway and said that once I got outside I'd wave up to the window. But once I got downstairs and outside, I heart the piano belting out a 'Scottish Selection'. She had already forgotten all about me and was hell-bent on livening up the melancholy-looking, lethargic lines of elderly inmates. This new purpose in life kept her going at first and she regained much of her confident and cheerful manner. None of these people had heard any of her stories, nor her repertoire of songs and tunes and she was able to work her way through the whole gamut. Soon she had gathered new stories, and the picture she used to paint of the house was invariably kind but often hilarious – the little romances that sprang up and how the ladies competed for the interest of a new gentleman resident. The fascinating lives some of the ladies had led in their youth. The sparkling wit of some of the gentlemen.

It always came as a shock to me when I visited my mother and she took me upstairs to the sitting room and I saw the lines of chairs facing the television, the rows of white heads and bent backs; the sadness of it all.

But the matron and my mother were great friends and my mother seemed to find comfort and security in this relationship.

It must have been a sad blow to my mother when that matron retired and left the city.

She remained to all outward appearances as cheerful as ever but her health deteriorated. She had 'internal troubles' which became progressively more painful and debilitating. Her strong, independent spirit began to clash with the new people in authority. She refused, for instance, to take the tranquillisers and sleeping pills that were dished out and that, as far as I could see, kept everyone half-asleep during the day and unconscious during the night.

I used to urge her to take them, pointing out that she was getting strained and anxious with lack of sleep. This, in turn, was causing headaches and all sorts of other distressing symptoms. The tranquillisers would make life easier for her (for *her*?) and soothe away her anxieties. But no, she wouldn't take them. It was a matter of defending her rights and her dignity as a free human being. Her spirit simply rebelled against joining those lines of zombies.

It made her an awkward ripple, however, in the smooth-running sleepy pond of a place.

When she became acutely ill she insisted on going to the hospital of *her* choice. She had been a believer in homeopathy for a lifetime and it was to the Glasgow Homeopathic Hospital that she wished to go.

Alternative treatment of this type is now perfectly acceptable. But then, the more traditional bastions of medicine (or at least some representatives of them) harboured a sneering and belittling attitude towards it.

I can remember when my mother returned from the hospital. She had to convalesce for a few days in the home's sick bay and I had come back with her in the ambulance and waited while she was comfortably tucked into bed by the matron.

Then, over my mother's bed, the matron read aloud the instructions the hospital had sent regarding treatment; and she tittered. I saw my mother's quick, hurt look and, frail though she was, she managed to speak up in defence of homeopathic treatment and of the Homeopathic Hospital. The matron adopted a subtle, patronising attitude, agreeing with her and treating her kindly as if she was an idiot child.

My mother made a few more pointed remarks backed up with facts and figures that showed she was anything but an idiot and, what's more, was not going to be treated like one.

She recovered enough strength to get up and about again and although she was now wrinkled and bent and her hair was thin as well as white, she could still step into the spotlight and put on a splendid act like the tough old trouper that she was. I would look out of my window in Bearsden and there she would be struggling along the road to come and visit me. We never missed a day of seeing each other. (She phoned me every day as well – often more than once.) If I couldn't get in to see her, she came to see me. If my husband was in, he would drive her back to the home in his taxi. Sometimes, on the way, he would buy her a box of sweeties. (His hatred of her and her hatred of him had long since petered out.) She had a terrible sweet tooth. Any kindness from anyone she appreciated wholeheartedly but specially any kindness from us.

I still have a letter here in my mother's dashing hand. (Her handwriting never became spidery or weak despite her age or physical weakness.) The letter, written after one occasion when my husband had given her a lift, says:

> I just had to write this letter to try to express my appreciation for your great kindness.
>
> I hope and pray that when your evening comes and Margaret's that you will both have the love and care that I have received from yourselves and I have faith you will. God hears

and knows even our unspoken prayers.

Thanking you once again, love, Mum.

I eventually moved from Bearsden to a flat only ten minutes' walk away from the home. I told myself and everyone that I needed to be nearer the Mitchell Library for research purposes and the house in Bearsden was too big and time-consuming to look after and I was getting into too comfortable a rut and it was affecting my writing. 'A place like Bearsden is death to a working-class writer,' I used to say. I even used to joke about having to move because I'd written a book about the place.

But looking back now, and struggling to be honest, did I not just move to be nearer my mother?

'One day,' I used to say to her, 'I'll make lots of money at my writing and I'll take you abroad on a holiday and you'll meet all sorts of new and interesting people and the sun will do you good.' (She had never been out of Britain in her life and, at this point, neither had I.)

But it was too late. She knew it and I knew it. She wasn't fit to go outside the home eventually. I think that must have been when I moved house. I knew how terrible it was for a woman of my mother's temperament not to get out and about. Like me, she loved the pulsating life of the city, and as well as visiting me, there was nothing she liked better than a jaunt into town every day. The La Scala restaurant was one of her favourite haunts. There, until she was no longer able, she often helped out as cashier when their regular cashier was off ill or on holiday or had left. It was like a second home to her and all the customers knew her. The public sitting room of the YWCA was another of her regular ports of call.

'There's lonely, sad folk in the YW that depend on me to cheer them up,' she used to say. 'They'd miss me if I didn't go in and have a wee blether with them and give them a tune.'

She always enjoyed a chat and laugh with Tommy, the old paper man at the corner of Sauchiehall Street and Hope Street too.

Once my mother couldn't get out, couldn't be independent, it was the beginning of the end for her. But her face lit up when I told her I'd found a flat near the home and could walk round and see her in ten minutes. I could see that she needed me to be near her to get reassurance from me. She seemed to pick anxiously at me all the time, searching out comfort. Her eyes would wilt with anguish and she'd say, 'Oh, Margaret, I hope Audley didn't think I didn't go in to see him sooner because I didn't want to see him . . .'

I would assure her for the hundredth time that Audley had asked that she didn't come into the hospital at first because he didn't want her to be worried or upset. He loved her and would never think anything wrong about her.

She would gaze at me tragically and say, 'There was that time when he was a wee boy and I left your daddy and took Audley with me and I found out afterwards that Audley had German measles. Maybe that harmed his heart. Trailing him away like that instead of keeping him warm in bed.'

Over and over again, I assured her that she'd been the best of mothers. No one could have been better.

'I kept remembering,' she said, 'how the poor soul suffered with the rheumatic fever.'

And I reminded her that since that time he had been happily married, travelled abroad and lived what life he'd had to the full.

'If only he hadn't been alone in that ward,' she said.

She also developed such a fearful anxiety in case anything happened to me. I walked every day from the flat to visit her and she'd phone me beforehand to make sure I was coming. Afterwards she'd phone to make sure I'd arrived safely back.

'Don't go out at night,' she'd say. 'These dreadful murders happen at night. The papers are full of all the horrors about them.' And she'd repeat all the horrors of the murders, and she'd keep repeating, 'Don't come the back way when you come to see me. Keep to the main street. There's a madman on the loose, remember. He could even strike during the day.'

Of course, the horrific murders were a general topic among everyone now. The serial killer even became another source of argument between my husband and me. My husband was for capital punishment. He had always been of the birch-them-and-hang-them school. I, on the other hand, had become involved with the Society of Friends (Quakers), who were against capital punishment and were also pacifists. When I say 'involved', I mean I occasionally went to Quaker Meeting for worship on a Sunday morning, if I could get away from the house. None of the Quakers knew anything of my difficulties or my unhappy predicament, but I felt comforted just by sitting among them. Even though sometimes the meetings were held in complete silence, I felt at peace and comforted by the silence.

My husband hated the Quakers and was furious at me having anything to do with them. He had been a bomber pilot during the war and was proud of it. He despised pacifists and 'weaklings'.

My mother agreed with him. He never swore in front of her but he did express his feelings and in support of him, she would remind me of what it said in the Bible, 'An eye for an eye...'

And her nagging anxiety about my safety on my daily journey to see her became an almost intolerable irritation. I began to dread my visits. And yet I wanted to see her. I longed to reach out to her and be at one with her. How can I explain the undercurrent of conflict, the seething turmoil of emotion that prevented me? I cannot. Not even to myself. Although, as a writer, I've got to keep trying.

31

My friend Ella used to make me laugh. She was brought up in Balornock and remembered my mother from those days. Ella enjoyed recalling old times.

'Remember,' she said, 'how your mother used to read teacups? She used to warn everybody that it was a lot of nonsense and she just did it for fun, but she was really good at it. My mother and I used to come round to your house and bring a bit of coal in our shopping bags because coal was rationed and my dad was the coalman, remember?'

It came back to me so vividly. My mother radiating pleasure at receiving the coal and immediately tossing it onto the fire and jabbing it about to make a cheery blaze. Then she'd fetch a pot of tea and a plate of gingersnap biscuits. We all had to take a biscuit and crack it against our elbows. According to my mother, if the biscuit broke in three pieces, it meant we would get a wish.

After the cup-reading, she would say, 'Now, come on through to the front room and I'll give you a wee tune.'

She would make us all sing. Ella said the only time she ever sang in her life was in my mother's house. The same applied to me and I couldn't sing any better than Ella. I could never even remember any words. But my mother would never take no for an answer. I had to find a song book in the piano stool and sing words from that.

Ella laughed until tears poured down her face, remembering.

'She never worried about housework or unmade beds or anything like that, your mother. "Och, the house will be here long after I'm gone," she always said. "Never mind the dirty dishes!" Then with a flourish on the piano, she'd close her eyes and launch with great feeling into, "I think that I shall never see, a poem lovely as a tree . . .'"

It was good recalling things like that. Happy things. Nights lying in bed with my wee brother in the darkness of the bedroom, listening to the reassuring sound of my mother's confident tread on the lobby linoleum as she went from living room to kitchenette and back, getting my father's supper ready.

Knowing she was there.

If only I could lay the ghosts of other nights. Where was I? Who was that woman who bathed me in a zinc bath by the side of an old-fashioned black range? The room is a pool of shadows and I instinctively know it is far away from Glasgow. I see myself standing in the bath. The woman has gone out of the room. A man is sitting on a fender stool very close in front of me. There is something in the way he is staring at me. I remember his eyes with fear, even today. I lower my head. I see the vulnerability of my pink skin. I try to find some numb place inside my head where I see nothing and feel nothing. The shadows envelop me and I am in another room in a hole-in-the-wall bed. In the darkness, in a strange, unknown place, I crouch back against the wall clutching the sheet over my mouth as I wait in terror.

Someone once said that all great writing is a bonus that comes from an unhappy experience. I don't know about that. Everyone has had unhappy experiences at some time or other but not everyone writes, and of those who do, few produce great writing.

They say everyone has at least one good book in them. I'm sure this is true. The challenge is in developing the characteristics necessary to write it. Many things go into the making of a novelist.

My brother made me a writer, and my father made me a writer, and perhaps most of all, my mother made me a writer.

I hear my friend Ella's laughter again:

Do you remember how your mother could count up pounds, shillings and pence in her head with the speed of light? Yet she could never remember anybody's street number. It never bothered her though, did it? She used to address letters in all sorts of queer ways like, 'Mrs Smith, the house with the bird bath in the garden, Cockmuir Street'. And it worked. Her letters always got there.

I remember. I remember my mother all ready to go out to play the piano at a very important function for which she was going to be paid. She was dressed in a long, bottle-green evening dress. God knows where or how she got it. But anyway, there she stood with proud dignity before us, back straight, handsome head held high, hands clasped in front of her waist displaying to advantage the delicate see-through sleeves with their patterns of coloured sequins. She wore no make-up. Her flushed cheeks and blue-black hair and brown eyes didn't need any enhancement.

She was beautiful.

How strange and confusing that my mother was much younger then than I am now.

We laughed together, Ella and I, as if it has always been laughter. Yet still, in my mind's eye, there is the bent, old woman.

I went into the home one day and opened her bedroom door without knocking and saw her for a few seconds before she realised I was there. She was up and dressed waiting for me to come but sitting on the edge of the bed with her thin legs dangling. Utter hopelessness had drained her face and eyes and she was gazing bleakly, tragically, into space.

The moment she saw me the spotlight turned on. She made

a conscious effort to straighten her shoulders and lift up her head. She smiled and began chatting to me.

And all the time she clung to her desperate optimism. Each time she became ill she spoke of going to the hospital as if she was off on holiday to visit old and well-loved friends. (She did love the doctors and staff at that Homeopathic Hospital.) All she needed was a change of surroundings for a wee while, she would say, and everybody in the hospital was so nice.

But once in, she would hear people moaning and crying out in pain and dying and it would make her think all the more of Audley. All she needed, she would say then, was to get back to the home among the old friends she'd made there. They were all so nice, and she missed them. But when she got back to the home, people were dying there too.

With each move she became frailer and weaker. And now she had angina as well as her other troubles. Then one day when I was kissing her goodbye, she clung round my neck and gazing up at me, said, 'If I could just stay a wee while at your place, I'm sure that's all I need to put me right.'

She'd always told everyone that I didn't want her to go into the home.

'There's always a welcome for me at Margaret's place,' she'd say. 'I didn't need to go into a home, you know. It was my idea, not Margaret's.'

Sometimes she'd turn to me for confirmation and say, 'Wasn't it?'

And I'd back her up with a firm 'Yes, of course.' But it was all part of the act. I thought she knew it.

Now, for the first time, she put me to the test.

'Oh no,' I said, 'I'd be afraid that you'd take one of your bad turns, Mummy, and I wouldn't know what to do to help you. You're far better here where there's the sick bay and the nurses and Matron just along the corridor.'

The light went out of her eyes. But she kissed me just the same.

I tried to make up for it on subsequent visits by becoming indignant when I learned that she hadn't a supply of tablets at hand to relieve her angina pain when it came on. My father used to always have some at hand so that when necessary he could melt one under his tongue. This relieved the angina spasm. My mother had to depend on someone hearing her cry out. I wanted to go along to the sick bay and put things right but she was now in such an apprehensive, anxious state, she didn't want to cause any trouble and she made me promise not to mention a word about it.

She was very lucky, she said, having her bedroom so near to the sick bay and everyone was really very nice.

By the time Christmas came and I told her that we'd collect her in the taxi and bring her out to our place for Christmas dinner, she wasn't able and instead had to spend Christmas Day in the sick bay.

I went to see her. She wasn't in bed. One of the small wards had been cleared and the dozen or so women patients had been placed in a semicircle in what looked like children's high chairs. Each had a tray fixed in front to pinion its occupant, who was further immobilised with a blanket tightly trussed round legs and feet. Shawls had been tucked over hunched shoulders and ludicrous paper crowns stuck on white heads.

Matron was going round untying bibs.

I looked at my mother. My beautiful, unique, courageous mother. Why did I not weep then?

Matron said how they were all having a lovely party and they'd all been very good and eaten up all their dinner.

My mother said, 'Margaret has a nice voice. She'll give you a song.'

I would have given anything at that moment not to let her down, to have been able to please her and make her proud of me. But I just couldn't remember any words. I couldn't sing.

'Of course you can,' my mother said.

But I couldn't.

She sang 'Bless This House' and immediately Matron began distracting everyone's attention by fussing with the old lady in the next chair, pulling her up and saying loudly, 'There you are, dear. That's better. That's a good girl.'

For a moment my mother gazed round at the Matron but her sweet, clear voice did not falter. She sang to the end of her song.

After that she was returned to her bedroom and I visited her there every afternoon as usual except on the occasion when I went to see her in the morning because I'd promised to visit a friend that afternoon. Morning or afternoon, her anxiety clung on to me. 'They've never caught that murderer yet, Margaret,' she'd say. 'Keep to the main road and phone me immediately you get home. I'll be sick with worry until I hear that you're still safe. Don't forget now, that serial killer is still on the loose.' She kept repeating this until I was beginning to feel almost as frightened and anxious as she was.

On the day I went to see her in the morning, she told me, 'One day that terrible pain is going to take me away. But I'm not afraid of dying because it will mean I'll see Audley again.' Her voice wavered a little. 'Won't it?'

I willed absolute certainty into my voice and eyes.

'Yes, Mummy, you'll see Audley again. I know you will.'

That was the last thing I ever managed to do for her. Later that afternoon I had a telephone call from the home asking me to come at once. When I arrived and went hurrying along the corridor towards her room, I saw the nurse waiting for me outside the door.

My mother was dead.

They asked me if I wanted to look at her, but I said no.

Now I wish I had seen her, just once again.

32

The flat that I was living in then was a comfort in a way. It was in a handsome redstone tenement looking on to a bank of trees and the Botanic Gardens. It was a nice peaceful outlook and yet, just beyond that, within a few minutes' walk, were the busy Great Western Road and Byres Road. Even just down from the tenement building in which I lived there were terraced houses and in one of them was the BBC Club. A few minutes away from there was the BBC's Broadcasting House.

The whole area was populated mostly with BBC people – actors, actresses and showbiz people – as well as the university population, because the university was also in that west end area. When we'd bought the flat, the previous owner had left the carpets and curtains which were all very good quality, and I found the colour – a soft, mossy green – calming and a pleasure to look at.

The place was handy for any of my friends to visit, with good public transport if anyone didn't have a car. It was especially handy for me because I didn't drive and I could get into the city centre to the big reference library quite easily or to any of the museums or art galleries.

The surroundings were pleasant and I had a room in which I could write. I threw myself into my writing so that I could cope with my grief.

While I was writing in that room, I was away in another world. It was only when I was perhaps sitting in the kitchen having a meal or walking down the street on my own en route to do some shopping that the grief would sweep over me and it was almost unbearable. It wasn't just the grief, of course. It was regret, it was guilt, it was thinking – if only if I had said this, if only I had done that. As far as real life was concerned, my relationship with my husband had deteriorated over the years until there was not only no sex, but no love, nothing. Nothing except his continual carping and criticism of me.

Someone once said that some people, to make themselves feel big, need to stand beside a dwarf and if they can't find a dwarf, they'll make one. That's what my husband was doing to me. He kept knocking me down, cutting me down, chipping away at my self-confidence, and the more successful I became as a writer, the more praise I received in that direction, the more he criticised me and made a fool of me.

Looking back now I can feel sorry for him because I believe he definitely felt my writing was a threat to him in some way. Nevertheless, I continued writing. I had parties in the flat with writer friends and my husband was always very polite to them and played the normal host, dishing out drinks to everyone and so on. But I don't think he ever felt at ease among that kind of people.

An awful thought occurs to me. Maybe I was subjecting my husband to the same kind of social torment that my mother inflicted on my father, although I can't honestly say that my husband was shy. Certainly not with any of his own friends. And he had regular men friends who visited the house far more often than any writer friends of mine. Nevertheless, it could be that he was lacking in self-confidence – indeed, I believe in spite of some of his arrogant behaviour towards me, he was a weak man, very much lacking in self-confidence.

As I've said before, we're all victims of victims and he once told me – not in the way of a complaint, quite the reverse, more of a boast about how capable his mother was – that he had been in some sort of a tantrum as a child and she had grabbed him by the hair, put him under the cold tap and run the water over his head. I was shocked at this and I still feel that that was a very wrong thing to do. He said it had definitely stopped the tantrum and shut him up. No doubt it did but I feel behaviour like that would be more liable to repress his ability to show emotion, because he was never able to show affection very easily. He never kissed or cuddled the children, for instance, or took them on his knee or showed any outward sign of affection for them, not even for Calvin.

Anyway, I didn't mean to cause him any unease when I invited my friends to the house. It was a case of survival with me. As I think I've said before, there must have been a strong bit about me because I just refused to be beaten, either in my writing or in my personal survival. He, at the beginning of our marriage, had said to me as he'd said to his first wife, that a married couple needed no one else but themselves, but very soon I realised what he really meant was that the wife should need no one else but the husband because he, right from the beginning, had his men friends but I wasn't supposed to have women friends.

At first I went along with that but not for very long. I soon went against that command that he gave me. It wasn't easy and he put up a real fight about it and made my life a misery, at the beginning especially, when I insisted on making, having and keeping friends. I became indeed very dependent on my friendships, almost as much as I was dependent for my survival and my sanity on my writing.

Then, suddenly, my husband announced that he'd seen a house out in a country area outside Glasgow and it was just the place for us. It was where Kenneth now lived with his wife. My husband said now that I had lost my mother, it would be a good thing for me to be nearer to Kenneth. In fact the last thing I wanted was to be emotionally dependent on Kenneth, or to be possessive or interfering in any way with his life. As far as I could see, Kenneth was getting on fine. Things were all right the way they were – we saw each other maybe once a week. He was getting on with his life and I was getting on with mine as best I could, which was as I believed it should be. If Kenneth had needed me in any way or for any reason, I would of course have made a point of being there for him.

Calvin by this time had been in the merchant navy and on a run in the Far East he'd met an Australian girl, married her and settled in Australia.

I tried to insist to my husband that I was a city person. I didn't want to live in the country. I wanted to continue living in the flat. He countered that he had never been used to tenements, he had always lived in a different kind of place. The inference was that, though I was used to the Glasgow tenements, he was used to better things and it wasn't good enough for him. I felt like reminding him about the poky wee council place opposite the gasworks that he'd lived in when I first met him. The building that we were now in was a beautiful place, in my opinion, and in such an attractive and interesting area.

Nothing worked, because he announced he'd already put in an offer for this property and had had it accepted. As a result, before I knew where I was, I was living in this country area in the middle of a new housing estate. It consisted of row upon row of tiny semis which all looked exactly the same.

It was a young population in that area, with young children. That was fine but it meant that there was nobody there of my generation. It was away from any shops and even away from any bus routes, so that in every way I felt isolated. It was a small house with only one public area downstairs which had to serve as both dining room and sitting area. There was a hatch into a tiny strip of kitchenette, and upstairs were the two small bedrooms and a bathroom. One bedroom was used as a storage area for boxes and extra furniture and so on, that had overflowed from our last, much larger house, and my husband refused to get rid of.

It meant that I could never have any friends in and relax with them and talk about writing or whatever interested us. We were always conscious of my husband being there and he was always there. It all became very awkward and my friends stopped coming as often. It wasn't convenient, anyway, for those of my friends who didn't have cars. I began to believe that my husband bought this house purposely to isolate me from my friends. However, his friends no longer came to visit us either. This touched me; I thought that he was giving up his friends in order to try and get closer to me and in his own way make the marriage a success.

I tried to feel grateful. I'd already had one failed marriage and I didn't want to fail at this one. I thought he was trying to change in order to please me. He even said he'd changed his mind about capital punishment and I had been right about that all along. I was touched at that too.

However, in desperation to get some time away from the claustrophobic atmosphere of the house, I took a part-time job in a Glasgow city centre shop.

One day during our coffee break, the other assistants and I were chatting about one thing and another and the subject got around to crime. One of the women remarked what a relief it had been when the serial killer was caught. While he'd been on the loose, it had been like a nightmare for every Glaswegian. No one knew who would be his next victim. I was astonished and confused. The assistants couldn't believe I hadn't heard.

'It's ages ago now. A year ago at least,' they said. 'It was on television and in all the papers. The whole trial and everything. How could you have missed it?'

I had no idea. It seemed impossible.

'He was as mad as a hatter, of course,' one of the women said. 'And he was detained at Her Majesty's pleasure.' That meant, apparently, that he was locked away for good in a half-prison, half-asylum place.

'Who was it?' I asked.

I wonder if anyone reading this can imagine the shock and horror I experienced when the name I was told was that of the young man my husband was friendly with. The young man I'd so often made welcome, shaken hands with, wished 'Happy New Year'. My stomach caved in. My blood seemed to drain from me. In my mind's eye, I saw this young man sitting quietly at our table, eyes down, eating the meals I so often had given him. Sitting with me and my children at the table, or by the fireside, always very quiet and smiling. This young man who knew when my husband was working at night and I was alone.

I felt myself having a nervous breakdown in retrospect. A jumble of thoughts crowded my mind. My husband must have used all sorts of devious ploys to prevent me seeing the television or the newspapers at the time. I couldn't think how he had done it – unless with all the busy time and worry about moving house. Maybe that was *why* he'd moved house. Now I realised that it hadn't been that he was trying to get closer to me and make a success of our marriage. Even his smarmy talk of how he had come to see that I had been right all along about capital punishment had been nothing to do with me. It was his friend he was thinking of. A terrifying thought struck me. Had he known all along what his friend had been doing?

I couldn't continue my work in the shop that day, or any other day. I left and went straight to the Mitchell Library and looked up back numbers of the newspapers.

And there it was – the whole story. Every day of the trial, every gruesome detail of the murders.

In a daze, I went home. I could hardly bear to speak to my husband. I didn't know what to say. My whole marriage, all the many stresses and horrors of it, weighed down on me more than it had ever done before. Now there was fear as well as horror.

193

'What's up with your face?' my husband asked, getting not only impatient but indignant. He had never ceased to insist that he had always been good to me. An ideal husband in every way. I was lucky to have him. He became really annoyed and reverted to his usual criticising and belittling of me.

I needed peace to recover from the shock I'd experienced so I tried to avoid giving him anything to latch on to but nothing worked. I kept going over and over everything that had happened in the past year. Surely he couldn't have known about the murders. No, bad and all as he could be as a husband, he wasn't a violent man. No, I couldn't believe he had anything to do with the murders, or had any previous knowledge of them. Nevertheless my nerves still felt shattered. Really shattered.

Then one day we were sitting in the narrow kitchenette at a shelf that served as a table. We were eating our lunch and for once he was silent but I knew from years of past experience that he would be trying to think of something to pick on me and nag me about. Nag, nag, nag. He'd been doing it for years.

Eventually he said, 'Do you see how many bananas there are in that bowl?' There was a bowl of fruit between us. I counted the bananas.

'Eight,' I said. 'Why?'

'There was four bananas in that bowl this morning,' he said, obviously getting into his stride, 'and you've gone out and bought another four.'

'So, we've lots of lovely bananas,' I said.

'That's you all over,' he got back at me. 'Spend, spend, spend!'

Now I'm not a person who uses bad language, I never swear and I'm usually a quiet-spoken person and, by this time, I'd become a Quaker. But this was the proverbial last straw. I'd put up with thirty years of God alone knows what from this man but this trivial incident was too much to bear. Far too much.

I suddenly got up and bawled at him, 'See you and your fucking bananas? You know where you can stuff them!'

He was horrified. 'Don't you dare use filthy language in my house!' he shouted back at me.

I didn't wait to hear any more. I grabbed my coat and my handbag and rushed out of the house. I ran and ran until I found a bus stop. I stood waiting for a bus, wondering where I was going to go and what I was going to do. One thing was certain, I had to do something. No matter what the truth was about him, I couldn't live with the man any longer.

Eventually a bus came along and I got on to it and went into town. I went to the office of a friend's husband who was a solicitor and I asked him how I could get a mortgage and he said, 'Well, I can try if you like, Margaret, but I haven't much hope. There's three things against you – your age, your sex and your job.'

It is different nowadays but that was the situation then. Women didn't seem to get mortgages, particularly more mature women, and also of course being a writer was a very insecure occupation as far as regular income was concerned. I left that office at absolute rock bottom in spirits. I couldn't face going back to the house or at least I had to delay it as long as possible.

I went to a café, ordered a cup of coffee and picked up a newspaper from the nearby rack. As I sipped my coffee, I idly leafed through the newspaper. I came upon a 'Flats to Rent' column and there was an unfurnished flat at what seemed a very reasonable rent. It didn't give an address for the house but it did give the name and phone number of the factor.

I contacted this factor immediately, was told that I needed two character references and a viewing time was arranged. I became feverishly excited and I thought probably everything would hang on the references. By this time, I knew the Maxwell Stuarts of Traquair House in the Borders. We met in connection with research and Flora read some of my work and became a fan. To cut a long story short, we became friends and still are to this day. Peter Maxwell Stuart died some years ago but at the time I was going for this flat, he was alive and well, and I phoned him and asked him if he would provide a reference for me. He supplied a really glowing reference.

I then contacted Quakers that I'd met at meeting for worship. One particular couple were titled people and the man, Lord Taylor of Gryffe, also sent me a wonderful character reference. Surely, I thought, two references like these would do the trick.

The area was one that was not familiar to me but, trembling with anticipation and increased fear because I was doing all this in secret without my husband knowing – indeed I didn't want him to know anything about it till it was all settled – I went to see the house. It turned out to be a main-door flat on two levels, with a lovely spacious, high-ceilinged hall, a big sitting room and bedroom upstairs, a curved stairway going down to a spare bedroom, bathroom, another large room, a big kitchen with dining area, and back door onto the back garden.

It seemed too good to be true, like a wonderful dream. It couldn't possibly happen to me. I just couldn't be this lucky. I still couldn't quite believe it when I got a letter from the factor saying I could have the house.

The next hurdle was how to furnish it. I hadn't enough money to buy anything. It would be a small miracle if I managed to pay the first quarter's rent. I went to the bank manager and convinced him that I was a potentially high earner with my writing. He knew of course that I was living in a bought house, which I suppose he'd regard as security.

With the money I got from the bank I furnished the house. But first of all I had to break the news to my husband. I remember standing in that wee kitchenette preparing something for our meal and I just suddenly said to him,

'I've got a flat.'

He said, 'What do you mean, you've got a flat?' He was always using that phrase 'What do you mean?' when I said anything. 'What do you mean, you've got a flat?'

'I'm leaving you,' I said.

'What do you mean, you're leaving me?'

'I'm leaving you,' I said, 'and I've got a flat to go to.'

'What do you mean, you've got a flat to go to?'

'I've found a flat to rent and as soon as I get packed tomorrow, I'm leaving here and going to live in the flat.'

A third degree ensued in which I told him where the flat was, something I wished later that I hadn't done.

Next day I packed my clothes and only my personal things – I never even took a teaspoon from the house – and I was ready to go. My husband insisted on giving me a lift to the place. He seemed to have turned quieter and more reasonable and I couldn't afford a taxi, so I agreed to go with him.

He'd never liked tenement buildings and had never wanted to live in one, according to what he'd told me previously, but when he saw this very nice red sandstone building in a nice tree-lined square and saw it was a main-door flat and not up a close, he was very impressed. He came in with me and wandered about, hands in pockets, jingling coins and puffing out his chest and looking, it seemed to me, rather proud and pleased with himself.

I could hardly believe my ears when he started saying things like 'I could put bookshelves along that wall' and 'I could have that bedroom downstairs'. In other words, he began talking as if he was going to move in with me. Shades of my mother, I thought. He's not paying a bit of attention to what I've said or what I want.

I had ordered different workmen to come right away, so a carpet-layer arrived, furniture that I had ordered arrived and before long there were a whole lot of men milling about the place, including my husband, who looked in his element. He disappeared for a short time and came back with planks of wood which he proceeded to put together as a two-shelf open bookcase that sat along one wall in the sitting room.

'There you are,' he said, 'that'll do for your books. Don't say I'm not good to you.' This was another phrase that he used quite often. I never had said that he wasn't good to me, in fact. He'd always been quite a DIY man and I suppose that was one of his good points because he always had done quite a bit of work around the house. At Christmas, he'd also made toys for the boys. I remember on one occasion he made a fort and that was one of Kenneth's presents.

Maybe with some other, different woman the marriage would have worked out in a different or better way. Maybe it was my fault that he was ignoring what I was saying now and ignoring the reality of the situation. Maybe it would have been better had I not kept quiet, not controlled my tongue so often. Maybe I should have shouted at him and sworn at him more often. Certainly, it seemed to me, he'd never liked the way I was and my recently joining the Society of Friends and becoming a Quaker had not helped the situation any.

If I'd been a good Quaker, of course, I wouldn't have needed to shout and swear. Quakers believe in speaking the truth but with love.

Now here he was working away along with the workmen who were attending to different jobs in my flat. The workmen obviously were taking it for granted that this was a perfectly normal situation – a husband and wife had got a new house and were getting it ready for them both to move in. They could think nothing else from the impression that my husband was giving them and the way he was talking.

Eventually, in desperation, because he was refusing to listen to what I was saying, I put it in writing. My letter was as terse and as abrupt as I could make it. To anyone reading the letter who didn't know the circumstances leading up to it, it could be said that it read as a cruel letter. I can't remember the exact words but it was very brief and said that the marriage was over, finished completely. I didn't want anything more to do with him. I didn't want him to come near me or my flat. I didn't want to set eyes on him ever again.

Knowing my husband and his capacity for self-pity, I could just imagine him showing Kenneth the letter, and even sending a copy to Calvin in Australia. Showing it in fact to anyone and everyone he could to prove how cruelly he'd been treated and what a cruel and uncaring person I was.

I certainly found out that he'd told Kenneth and others that he wasn't a bit surprised when he got my letter because he'd always known that as soon as I became successful as a writer, I'd get rid of him. This was the worst thing about me leaving, as far as I was concerned.

I felt so sad that Kenneth might feel more sympathetic to the man he'd always called Dad than to me and that he wouldn't understand the real reasons behind the break-up of our marriage. In order to give Kenneth and Calvin as secure and stable and loving a background as possible, I had always tried my best to hide any disagreements or unhappiness in my marriage. I'd always tried to keep my temper. There had been the odd occasion when just a trivial thing my husband would say (like the outburst before I left, though maybe not as strong) would make me burst out with what would appear to be an unfair and harsh retort. In fact it would have been a last straw in a build-up of irritations, resentments, fears and all sorts of pressures and tensions inside me.

I remember on one such occasion we were all sitting at the table having a meal and I had burst out with something. Kenneth turned to me and said 'Mum!' in a surprised, shocked and reproachful way.

A few years after the divorce, when my husband had been in hospital, my son phoned me up and said, 'Mum, I'm afraid I've got bad news for you.'

'What?'

'Dad has died.'

I said I was very sorry to hear it. Then his voice broke and he said, 'I wish I could have got on better with him.'

I told Kenneth that his dad had just been a difficult man and that, in fact, Kenneth had got on better with him than Calvin had. Kenneth had been a good son to my husband, there was no doubt at all about this. Right up to the end, he'd done his best and been a comfort to him. He'd visited him every day in hospital and had been with him when he died.

After our divorce, my husband had decided to go over to Australia to live with Calvin. Before he got all his business completed and everything in order, he stayed with Kenneth for a few weeks and Kenneth and his wife had been as welcoming and as hospitable to him as they could. After he'd gone over to Australia, he had bought a house for Calvin in which they both lived for a few months, but he didn't get on with his son and eventually returned to Scotland and lived for a time with a brother of his.

Kenneth continued to keep in touch with him and did all he could to help him and so I was perfectly sincere when I told Kenneth that he had been a very good son indeed. I asked him that time on the phone when he told me about my husband's death if I ought to go to the funeral. He said, 'No, I don't think so, Mum. It would just upset you.'

So I agreed not to go but I sent a wreath of flowers, with a card on it which said 'In remembrance of times past' (which was from Proust), I was meaning the times past that had been happy times – occasional days at the seaside in the summer, Christmas Day and all the excitement of opening presents, birthday parties, times when he had been kind to my mother after she had become ill and grief-stricken.

I had always dreaded in a way hearing of my husband's death because I wondered if I would be overcome with a panic of regret and guilt and be sad and upset beyond measure. I did feel genuinely sorry for his sake when I heard the news of his death but the only other thing I felt was like my mother after my father died when she said, 'Oh, the pity of it.'

I thought in the same way about his friend and what had happened in his family. I remembered what I'd heard about his father from another friend of my husband and how it had given me a glimpse of how he had suffered terribly as a child and was probably still suffering. I felt desperately sorry for the victims of his crimes and sad at the thought of how much damage can be caused within families, then spread out to affect other people so tragically. I once heard a talk given by a prison psychiatrist who had worked with serial killers and he said every murderer he'd ever dealt with had been subjected to abuse and some sort of torment as a child.

I was lucky – I had been abused and tormented but I always had my writing as a form of therapy. So many abused and unhappy people have nothing.

33

Something very unexpected happened some time after my husband's death. My son came to me and said, 'Mum, would you mind if I tried to find my real father?' I'd always been honest with Kenneth and as soon as he was old enough to understand, I had explained that I'd been married before and that was when he was born.

I told him I had no objections but didn't know how he would go about it. I'd heard nothing about my first husband for many years. I'd never seen him or heard anything from him directly but I had kept in touch and remained friendly with his mother. She had told me that he'd left the navy eventually, gone into the river police in London, married again and had a family – a son and, I thought, two daughters. When his mother died, I never heard anything more about him.

Kenneth said that he would try the Salvation Army but they told him that George, my first husband, wasn't a missing person as such and it wasn't a case that they could deal with. Then Kenneth tried the chief of the Metropolitan Police in London and that was successful. One day my daughter-in-law phoned me up and said, 'Ken's away to work and he's terribly excited – though he's pretending not to be – because he's just had a letter from his real father.'

The letter had said that he was surprised and delighted to hear from Kenneth and could they meet – suggesting date and time – at the ticket barrier at Waverley Station in Edinburgh. The day of the meeting was a Saturday and I went over to Ken's house and his wife and I waited with great interest and suspense for Ken's return to hear how he'd got on.

Ken had said before he left – trying to be very laid-back – that all he was worried about was whether his real father had gone bald because balding was hereditary. It turned out that George still had a good head of hair but of course there was far more to it than that.

When Kenneth came back, he was still trying to look cool and unemotional and, when we asked how he'd got on, he shrugged and said, 'All right.' Eventually we got him to start talking and he said that, in actual fact, it had been a terribly emotional meeting.

'Oh, well, he hasn't seen you since you were a baby, son,' I said.

He replied, 'No, it was more than that. We went to a hotel to have a drink and talk and he was weeping. He told me that his son had been killed in a motorbike accident and he'd been a broken man, on a bottle of whisky a day. Then, out of the blue, after thirty-odd years, came a letter from his other son.'

If I had put that in a novel, it would have looked contrived and unbelievable – too much of a coincidence. Truth really is stranger than fiction.

So Ken visited George and his family regularly and they visited Ken's home regularly. Ken and George got on really well together and Ken liked him. George's wife must have been a very nice person indeed because she accepted Ken into the bosom of her family. Ken told me that George had said, 'I was a very foolish young man, Ken. Do give your mother my kindest regards.' And I reciprocated. I was so happy and grateful that Ken had become part of this stable, secure, loving and happy family network (he now had three half-sisters). Sadly, George is now dead, so Ken has lost two dads.

Before that sad occasion, however, my friends (and fans) in Traquair House, Flora and her then husband Peter Maxwell Stuart, suggested that I write something about one of their ancestors. Peter was a charming man. Now Flora has recently married again to another lovely man. But at the time I'm talking about, Peter was still alive. The ancestor they spoke of was a woman called Mary Ravenscroft, who was the wife of one of the earls of Traquair. I wasn't in the habit of being given characters like this. I liked to do my own thing, to think of ideas myself and become excited about them and about the characters that the story would involve. I explained this to my friends and Flora said, 'Well, come and see the research material we have here and maybe that'll get you excited.'

So I went through to Traquair and I was not shown into the big museum part that had a chest of all sorts of papers and manuscripts and charters, but into another private room and it was filled with letters and diaries and journals. It was an absolute goldmine, a treasure trove for any writer or researcher. I couldn't resist accepting the suggestion of writing this book.

Four main things went wrong in the process. One was the fact that there was so much research, I got quite overwhelmed by it.

Another reason was that, although I was quite fascinated by the life and the people that the research material depicted, at the same time I couldn't really identify with them, especially with Mary Ravenscroft. I could admire her, but I couldn't quite summon up enough personal identification with her, see into her with that intimate identification that I normally could with other characters I'd written about. A lot of the journals, letters and diaries made references to money, or rather the lack of it, and were pleading poverty at a time when they had nineteen servants, for instance. I tended to roll my eyes at this sort of thing when I read it. Of course, I appreciated that poverty was a relative thing and no doubt they didn't have much cash, particularly compared with some other members of the gentry that they knew at the time. Also of course, with nineteen servants, it meant all these mouths to be fed, because the servants all had to be kept by the Traquairs.

The third difficulty was that I kept imagining Flora and Peter Maxwell Stuart looking over my shoulder all the time, breathing down my neck. Of course, they weren't. They were giving me perfect freedom to do what I liked, but it was just the way I felt. I kept thinking that I had to please them, indeed I wanted to please them because I was very fond of them. This was all inhibiting as far as my writing was concerned. I would come to a part where I thought there should be a sexy scene and then I'd think, 'Oh, better not say that in case I would embarrass Flora or Peter.' After all it was their family, their ancestor that I was writing about and they might not want me to go into such intimate detail for everyone else to read.

My fourth difficulty was in having the main character a real person – not just the model, not just making a fiction modelled on a real person, but actually the real person. I wanted to do justice to this woman, to create a really truthful picture of her. But how could I when she revealed so little about herself? She had left diaries, that was true, but strangely enough, she revealed nothing of her thoughts and her emotional life in the diaries. They only gave a factual account of what had happened, or the duties that she had to do, or the places she had to visit – factual things like that which as a novelist weren't nearly so important to me as how the woman had actually felt about her life, about her family, and about the people around her.

I plodded on with the book as best I could. Halfway through it, however, I felt instinctively that it had gone wrong. I sent what I'd written to the publisher and instead of sending me a rejection slip, or a letter telling they didn't want to publish it, the head of the publishing firm, at that time a woman called Rosemary Cheetham, actually flew up from London and arrived at my house to say that rather than write me a letter or phone me, she wanted to tell me to my face what she thought was wrong with this book.

I really appreciated that. I thought it so kind of her to take this trouble for me. But before she could say any more, I said to her, 'Well, can I tell you first of all what *I* think is wrong with this book?' I proceeded to tell her and she said, 'That's spot on, Margaret. That's exactly what's wrong with it.'

I said to her, 'Well, let's forget that book. Here is a synopsis I've written for another book.' I handed her an outline of a book that I had thought up, a book set early in the twentieth century, in the middle of the First World War, and I had called it *Rag Woman, Rich Woman*. She read the synopsis there and then, and looked up at me and said, 'Margaret, that sounds wonderful! That's the book we'll have instead.' We had a nice lunch together, spoke about other things and then she flew back to London. I abandoned the Traquair book, although I still have it in the house somewhere and maybe one day I'll go back to it and write it again. Or rather, I'll write a novel and use Traquair House as a setting for some of the scenes.

Meanwhile I immediately got down to work on *Rag Woman, Rich Woman*. I felt far more at home now and I could identify with all of the characters in the book. They became real to me and eventually real to the reader – I know that because I had so many letters from readers who had thoroughly enjoyed the book.

I'll never forget how nervous I was about going to the first night of *Rag Woman, Rich Woman* when it was performed on the stage. After I had written the book and it was published, I wasn't at my readers' elbow when they finished the book. They might toss it aside and say it was a lot of rubbish. Thankfully I wouldn't know about that. But to go to a theatre, you get an immediate response from the audience. I feared they might boo the performance and the story at the end of the evening.

As it was, it was a great success but one thing that really astonished me at the time was one scene in the play which had been in the book. All of a sudden in the middle of this scene, a woman two or three rows in front of me got up, crushed along the row and just got to the aisle in time to collapse. She was stretched out on the floor and had to be carried out. Over at the other side of the theatre, I heard a clatter. I looked round just in time to see a woman sliding down under the seats. In fact, several people fainted during the performance and had to be helped out. I thought this was absolutely disastrous and when I was leaving – slinking out – at the end of the performance, one of the doormen who recognised me spoke to me. I said to him, 'Oh, that was awful. Did you see the people fainting?'

'Did you know who one of the women was?' he asked.

'No,' I said.

'The drama critic of *The Herald*!'

I thought she would either ignore the play in the paper next day or she would slate it. When I got home, I called a friend who was also a writer but who couldn't come to the first night. I said to her, 'Oh, Evelyn, it was a disaster. There were people fainting and being carried out.'

She said to me, 'You lucky devil! What wonderful publicity!' This hadn't occurred to me but of course she was right. The play got excellent reviews and played to packed houses. The sales of the book shot up. Even that drama critic of *The Herald* was generous in her review.

At the beginning of *Rag Woman, Rich Woman* I had put 'This book is dedicated to the loving memory of my father, Samuel Thomson'. He had been the model of different characters in different books already, of course. Each time I'd taken a part of him, one characteristic, and concentrated on that, exaggerating it even, and adding to it other different characteristics, which in the end created a new fictional character, but at the same time keeping to the true essence of the real character, or what I thought was the true essence at the time.

After my father died, however, I found dozens of diaries and journals he'd written in secret. Especially in the journals were the outpourings of the inner man and of course, it's the inner man who's of most interest and concern to the novelist.

Here in these diaries and journals was a man I had never known but now, knowing him, a thousand confusions, resentments, hatreds, emotional traumas that I'd endured all my life were suddenly thrown into a melting pot. New emotions crowded in to take their place and these new emotions were totally unendurable. Here was a painfully shy, lonely human being who found it difficult to communicate with others but found solace by communicating with himself by writing. I suppose if anyone dies, the family who are left feel, to some degree or other, if only – if only I'd said this, if only I'd done that. Added to these feelings, I kept thinking, if only I'd known. If only I'd known so many things, but especially the fact that he was a writer.

In *Rag Woman, Rich Woman* and in future books, I either expressed my father's feelings by quoting his exact words from his journal, or I put them into third person narrative form. One way or another, with the help of his own writing, I expressed his feelings in *Rag Woman, Rich Woman*, especially the chapter that describes him as a young man when he first meets my mother. It also, I believe, gives a poignant insight into his character and his life.

34

I felt I had to continue the story of Matthew (the character based on my father), Rory and her family and friends too, and of course Victoria, who were all in *Rag Woman, Rich Woman*. And so I wrote a follow-up. That was the book that became *Daughters and Mothers*.

By this time I had discovered that, far from being the stupid, hopeless, useless creature who would never be able to cope on her own that my husband had always insisted I was, I could in fact cope very well. I didn't mind my own company, I wasn't even lonely. Well, there were occasions when I took temporary little panics of aloneness. They would happen if I had been out visiting friends and had a happy evening chatting to them or I'd had a happy and busy evening at a speaking engagement where I had been surrounded by readers asking questions and getting me to sign copies of my books for them.

Afterwards, I would come home to the silent empty house and I would have one of these flutters of panic but I'd go straight to the television and switch it on. It gave an illusion of company. The sound of the voices and the pictures on the screen would calm me. Other than that, if I felt troubled at all, I only needed to go into my writing room and soon I was surrounded by my imaginary people and how could I feel lonely then?

My writing room had shelves all round the walls, right up to the ceiling, packed with books that I had got for research purposes, but I'd very soon found what type of research I enjoyed doing most. That was speaking to people. Speaking to people about their jobs, speaking to elderly people about their memories of times past, chatting to all sorts of people – or rather they chatted to me and on to my tape-recorder, if I had arranged an interview with them. People, I'd long since come to realise, were my raw material. But apart from that, I just love people. I don't drive so I use public transport and I walk about the streets, keeping my eyes and ears open, especially on buses, and I never have any difficulty finding characters or material for my books. Especially in Glasgow. Glasgow is just hotching with characters. Like the time I was sitting on a bus and I overheard two mature ladies who were sitting in front of me complaining about the amount of sex there was on television these days. Eventually one of them said, 'Aye, ye're quite right, Sadie. Ah'd far rather dae it than watch it.'

Another two Glasgow matrons in a bus and one of them said to the other, 'I don't like these see-through nighties. They show your vest.'

Another day a woman saved me from wandering dreamily under a bus by grabbing me and jerking me to safety with the words 'Ye nearly got yer coat pressed there, hen!'

I knew these women and many others were potential characters for my stories, even the ones I'd glimpsed in passing. Henry James, talking of this kind of novelist's knowledge, said it was 'the power to guess the unseen from the seen'.

I mentioned giving talks. I get asked more and more to do this and I enjoy doing it, whether it's in libraries talking to people, most of whom have read my books, or talking to writers' clubs in an effort to help beginner writers. Sometimes I get really busy spells of giving talks and I remember one time, when I'd given a talk and a woman caught me just as I was hurrying away into a dark and rainy night in order to catch a taxi home. She said she hadn't had the chance to have a proper talk with me, there had been so many people at the meeting asking me questions. She asked if I could meet her at a hotel in town the next morning for a coffee. In my harassment I said OK, and then she asked if she could bring a friend who was a great fan of mine and who was dying to meet me. Again I said OK although I was up to my eyes in work and hadn't really the time to meet anyone for coffee, or anything else.

Next day, while we were waiting for her friend to arrive, she mentioned that he wasn't really a friend at all (I later discovered that he wasn't really a fan of mine either). Apparently she had met this man on a train travelling from Glasgow to Edinburgh and they'd got talking. I think between Haymarket and Waverley stations she told him that she knew a writer and he told her that he'd written a book. Eventually the man arrived with a pal. He was obviously wanting to make a foursome. He also had a case. This he opened as soon as he sat down and revealed it to be full of the manuscript of his book. He said he wanted me to take it home and read it and let him know what I thought of it and which publisher he should send it to. I said I'd have to deny myself the pleasure of reading his manuscript as I was up to my eyes in a book I was writing myself.

After an hour or two of him telling me about the story, I managed to make for the door but trying to be kind, I said en route, 'Well, I wish you well with your book. You don't want to be like Van Gogh who didn't make his millions until after he was dead.'

His pal said, 'Aye, Margaret's right. Poor old Van Gogh never sold one book before he died!'

Some people, some writers in particular, believe that everything they need to know is in books. I know it can be done. I know writers who have done it very well by using reference books alone as sources of their research. But I personally feel that there's always an added something – something that brings the novel to life in a more vivid and authentic way – if you go to the place you want to write about,

211

if you can experience it, if you can observe the people in it, if you can talk to them. If you experience and observe first-hand in your own personal way, not anyone else's, in your very own honest way of looking at life and people, there lies your fresh approach and your originality.

Obviously, if you're writing about previous centuries there isn't anyone around that can tell you about their experiences and life at that time and then you have to depend on written material. The best kind, though, I find for that is letters and journals. That's the next best thing to the people speaking to you.

Daughters and Mothers started in 1945 so of course I could speak to people who remembered that time. I remembered it myself too but I had to speak to as many people as possible. It was the time of the Cold War too and I felt at the time, if only ordinary people here could get to know ordinary people over in what was then the Soviet Union, surely it would help matters.

I believe that one of the functions of a good novel is to create bridges of understanding between people. First and foremost it must be a good story and it must be entertaining, but at the same time, if the novelist can create some sort of understanding and even compassion for different kinds of people, even in some small way, then that is an extra and surely valuable function.

Anyway I decided that I wanted to find out more about the people in Russia for myself and be able to reflect whatever I found out through the characters that I had in my novel. I decided to make one of the characters in the novel, Donovan, who was an investigative reporter, get an assignment to go over to the Soviet Union to find out what the place and life were like. Because his daughter Helena is rather spoiled and has been getting into trouble in Glasgow, it is decided that he'll take her with him to get her out of this problem situation she's in in Glasgow.

On the plane going over I met Jimmy, an elderly gentleman who had been going to the Soviet Union every year on holiday since the early fifties. This of course would be the very time that Donovan and Helena would be going over and so I asked Jimmy if he would tell me all about his experiences of the Soviet Union and the people. He told me that he spoke fluent Russian and had made many friends among the ordinary folk. I was delighted when he agreed to tell me all he knew about the country and people onto my tape-recorder. When we arrived at the hotel and after we got unpacked, we met in the lounge and looked around for a quiet spot in which I could use my tape-recorder, but it was a very busy hotel and eventually I said to him, 'Well, if you wouldn't mind, Jimmy, you could come up to my bedroom.'

He didn't mind at all and up he came, but I soon discovered there was no problem in getting him to talk. The problem was getting him to stop talking. He talked and talked and talked for hours. I was getting exhausted and eventually I asked him, 'Jimmy, do you never get tired of talking?'

He replied, 'Well no, Margaret. You see, my wife doesn't allow me talk at home so I like to try and enjoy myself when I come on holiday.'

He was still enjoying himself talking as I eased him towards the door. I opened the door eventually and got him out into the corridor. It was pretty late by this time but there were still quite a few people going about. There was a Buddha-type lady sitting in the hallway outside – I don't what their purpose was but at that time there was always one of these women on each floor of the hotel. When I got Jimmy to the door, he suddenly called out in a voice like a foghorn, 'Oh, Margaret, that was great. I thoroughly enjoyed that. Thanks very much.'

I saw everybody looking round and wasn't sure what kind of reputation I'd have after that.

During my travels in the Soviet Union, I met many people and made lots of friends. There was one hotel I was staying in where a man came to the hotel from Moscow to answer any questions the foreigners might have about life in the Soviet Union. His name was Mikhail Lubimov.

An English tourist asked him why it was that so many of our people were over staying and holidaying in hotels in the Soviet Union but nobody from his country seemed to be over in Britain on holiday in any of our hotels, and particularly not in any private houses in Britain. Lubimov asked this man what the average wage was in Britain and when the man gave a figure, Lubimov gave the average wage in the Soviet Union, which was about a quarter of the British figure. He said, 'That is why our people are not over in your country having holidays either in hotels or private houses.'

I was a bit suspicious of this so I said, 'Does that mean if I offered free hospitality to, for instance, a Russian writer, they would be allowed to come and spend time in my home?'

He said, 'Yes.' So I handed him my card and said, 'Well, I'm offering free hospitality for a Russian writer.'

Nothing more was said and I went back home to work on my book. Before returning home, though, I had been having a problem because I wanted some sort of model for the Russian hero that I was going to have in the book and so far no one that I had seen had inspired me. But one day I was sitting in the bar of this particular hotel on my own and a waiter approached me to take my order. As soon as I saw him, I thought 'That's the one!' There was just some sort of chemistry about him, something about his eyes and the way he walked that made me decide that he was the model for Burgeyev in my book, *Daughters and Mothers*. I came home eventually and got on with the writing of the book. I became so immersed in this that I forgot all about the incident with Mikhail Lubimov. Then, all of a sudden, I started getting letters, telegrams, phone calls from the Writers' Guild in Moscow. Lubimov had contacted them and they had arranged for what they said was a very famous writer to come and visit me.

All my friends thought I was mad. Of course they'd often flung up their hands in horror when they'd heard about some of the people that I got talking to, invited to my home, and became friends with, even in Glasgow. The day came and I went to the airport and stood waiting for my guest's flight to come in. I stood with a piece of cardboard with my name on it held above my head. I saw this lady coming smiling towards me and I knew right away that we would become good friends, which indeed we did. And of course she was the first of many overseas friends who visited me.

An interesting point about this story, though, was that Mikhail Lubimov kept in touch with me. He wrote to me and asked how I was getting on with my Eastern guest. I wrote back and told him. He wrote to me and told me different things he was doing and I wrote and told him what I was doing. We became pen-pals and at one point he wrote and said that he wanted to become a writer and I wrote back giving him some hints and tips. These letters went back and forth every few months, and continued for a number of years. Then one day I had an unexpected phone call from Mikhail.

'I'm speaking from London just now, Margaret, but I've to go back to Moscow in the morning. I just wondered if you'd seen the article about me in the *Sunday Telegraph*.'

I don't get that paper so I said, 'No.'

Then he told me that it explained about his KGB work. Well, you could have knocked me down with the proverbial feather. I dashed out next day to the Mitchell Library to try to get the previous day's paper. They didn't have it. I then phoned the *Telegraph*'s head office in London and they sent me a copy. Here was his photograph splashed across the page and underneath it was quite a big article about him. Colonel Mikhail Lubimov, head of KGB British Section. He was the man that recruited all the famous spies from Britain and his book on the British personality apparently was required reading for the KGB. I thought, please

God, don't tell me I helped him to write it. I wrote to Mikhail and told him what I thought of the article and ended my letter with what I thought was a joking, throwaway line. I wrote, 'I'm now grappling with the problem of how to fit a KGB colonel into my Glasgow-based family saga.'

He wrote back and told me exactly how I could do it, gave me in fact a brilliant story line. I've never used that story line because it was a spy story and I don't like spy stories. I never read them and I certainly had no notion of writing one.

I found out other information about Mikhail from other subsequent articles. Apparently he'd been chucked out of the KGB because, for one thing, he seemed to have too many westernised ideas and also because he was a supporter of Gorbachev. As soon as Gorbachev went out of favour, so did Lubimov.

I've long since lost touch with him but I believe he is now an established writer. I read somewhere that he's had a couple of best-sellers in America and another two books are in the pipeline. He's been on a lecture tour in the USA. I've also heard he's given lectures to tourists on a pleasure ship that sails on the River Volga – to mention just a few of his achievements since leaving the KGB.

Meeting so many different kinds of fascinating people is one side of being a writer that makes life so interesting for me. I have been laying great emphasis on people and speaking to people and how this is so important to me. Words are important too, of course, to a writer. We should always try to use the right words, the exact words, to convey our meaning.

When Dr Johnson's wife found him in bed with his chamber maid, his wife said, 'I'm surprised.'

'No,' Dr Johnson said, 'you are not surprised. We are surprised. You are astonished.'

Yes, getting the words right is important. And I haven't always got them right. I remember one time I was at an antique book fair – I spend a lot of money buying second-hand and antique books to help with my research. Anyway, at this particular book fair, I met an awfully nice American man. We were getting along so well. My mother would have said we 'clicked'. At one point, he told me he was a genealogist and I immediately launched into the details of my hysterectomy.

Wrong word! Unclicked!

Another time I remember getting the wrong word was when I was describing to a friend my visit to a church. It was full of incest, I told him. 'That must have been interesting,' he remarked.

However, to me *the* most important element of my work is people. I'm interested in them, I'm curious about what makes them tick.

35

After travelling round the Soviet Union and meeting and speaking to as many people as I could, I came to the conclusion that although it was a vast country of infinite variety – its terrain, its climate, its language, its religion and its people – the people, fundamentally, were just the same as anyone I'd ever met in Scotland, or in Britain, or anywhere else for that matter. They wanted to love, and to be loved, they wanted to be able to feed themselves and their families, they wanted a decent roof over their heads, they wanted to be happy and they wanted to live in peace.

I was later to get the very same impressions in America although it was a different place from the Soviet Union in many ways. Yet there was a strange similarity I felt between the two nations. My first travels in America came to pass when I was doing research for my book, *Wounds of War*. This was to be a story not about the war, not set at the time of the war, but it was to be about the fact that war could have its effect on people years and years after the conflict had taken place.

I wanted to set the book in the sixties and when I had started my research I was reminded that that was the time of the Civil Rights movement and Martin Luther King in America. That's what decided me to travel over to America to get first-hand impressions and talk to people who'd actually experienced this part of history. I was helped in this by an American friend that I was awfully fond of. Her name was Betty Turnell.

How that came about was the Scottish Tourist Board had had a request from Betty, who was an elderly unmarried lady.

She was a professor and she had been touring around Europe studying broadcasting methods in different countries. She had already travelled around England and now she was in Scotland. She had some interviews to do with the BBC in Glasgow. She was so fed up with living in hotels, however, that she had contacted the Tourist Board and asked if she couldn't be placed in a private home in Glasgow for the duration of her stay.

I remember thinking what a courageous lady she was because Glasgow at that time had a dreadful reputation for violence and gangsters. This had come mainly from the book *No Mean City: a Story of Glasgow Slums*. That book in my opinion had given a very wrong impression of Glasgow. I'm not criticising the writing, the character creation or the story – it's a long time since I've read it now, but I believe it was quite a riveting story with quite strong characterisation. But it gave the impression that everyone in Glasgow was either in a gang or going about with a razor up their sleeve. I had been brought up in Glasgow and I'd never seen anyone with a razor nor witnessed a gang fight. Indeed, I'd always found such warmth and friendliness in the Glasgow people. No doubt there had always been an element of violence and of course there had been gangs at loggerheads at times, but it wasn't a general kind of thing in Glasgow, any more than in any other big city. Every big city has some element of crime and Glasgow is certainly no worse than any other city – a lot better than many, in fact.

I admired the pluck of this elderly lady requesting to live in a private home when she came for her first visit to Glasgow. The Tourist Board contacted me because I was a writer and particularly because many of my short stories by this time had been broadcast on BBC Radio. They had the impression we had something in common.

Betty duly arrived at my house and she was a delightful lady. She was really small in stature – she couldn't have been over five feet, a tiny, delicate-looking, wee creature. We got on very well and she stayed for some time and I showed her around Glasgow. She thoroughly enjoyed her stay and came back the following year with her sister for a holiday. They both stayed with me and we travelled around quite a bit. It was such a pleasure seeing her again and she insisted that I came over to America and allowed her to return the hospitality.

When it came to doing research for *Wounds of War*, I wrote to Betty explaining my situation but said it would be mostly in the Deep South that I would need to do my research. I got a phone call from her saying she would see to it I got all the information I needed. She offered to drive me around different parts and end up by going to the southern states. She met me at the airport and because I hadn't seen her for some time, it took me by surprise to see just what a tiny, frail-looking wee thing she was. Now she also had a stick because she'd fallen not long before and broken her leg. I could hardly credit the fact that she was going to drive me all around America.

The first place she took me to was to visit some relations of hers. I used Betty as the model for Aunt Abbie in *Wounds of War* and I not only characterised her in the book but I described her driving in some detail. After the book was published I sent Betty a copy and, of course, sometimes I get fact mixed up with fiction and I'd forgotten (or never consciously realised) how close Aunt Abbie in the book was to the real-life character.

Poor Betty wrote back and said she surely had not been such a dreadful driver as I portrayed her in the book. I was so upset in case I had offended her that I had to write back straight away, trying to explain how I fictionalised and exaggerated any characteristics that I wrote about. I added quite a lot of imagination, I explained, so that I always created perfectly different and new characters that bore very little relation or resemblance to the original trigger for the character. I hope she forgave me.

36

Before Betty and I set off for the southern states, she took me to her home. Betty's place was in a street lush with overhanging trees. It was a wooden bungalow. Inside it seemed very dark at first – all the blinds were down and of course the overhanging porch keeps the sun from inside too. I discovered that was the idea and a very necessary idea to keep the house shady.

The house was furnished with antique furniture, a beautiful rocking chair and embroidered seated chairs. In the bedrooms there were patchwork bedspreads on beds that her grandfather had carved. The first words Betty said to me when we set foot over her threshold were, 'This is your home, Margaret.' She was really such a lovely person.

Later that first day in her home she had a phone call from an ex-student who now owned several radio stations and flew his own plane. He invited us to meet him for dinner at the airport restaurant. He turned out to be a very high-powered guy, the kind who literally flies from one appointment to another. As soon as the meal was finished, he began looking at his watch. He was a good-looking man with dark hair and moustache and he kept staring straight at me, pinning me down with his stare when he asked questions about my books and writing. At the same time he was kind and polite and he was obviously very fond of Betty.

She must have been a wonderful teacher – so many of her students keep in touch and have done well. The man who was running for Vice-President of America at the time was an ex-pupil. I can't be certain because so many of her ex-pupils were famous people but I have a sneaking feeling he was the one she'd confided hadn't been a very bright pupil. She hastily added that he was a very nice young man and he'd gone far and been very successful – all credit to him. She reminded me that Churchill had apparently been a slow developer and not terribly bright at school either.

Everywhere we'd gone so far and now everywhere we went in her home town, Betty took with her a bag of my books. I was embarrassed but at the same time grateful. She determinedly plugged me at bookstores, libraries, universities, newspaper offices and radio stations. Everybody was very polite and friendly towards me. In one bookshop, a woman said to me, 'Welcome to our country and have a nice day.'

Another woman in a jeweller's shop was so effusive, she seemed to bend forward with the size and weight of her smile and her efforts to assure me of good service and friendliness.

We went to the bank where Betty had to do some business and also she wanted me to meet Wanda, the lady in charge of the bank, who was also a friend of hers and who had already called to invite us to lunch. I found Wanda very charming and kind, but very high-powered, and obviously used to getting what she wanted. She had straight, short white hair, very well cut and a good tanned complexion. She was expensively made up and mascaraed and had long, pink-painted, perfectly shaped nails. On her hands were at least five or six large, flashing diamond rings and she wore equally sparkling diamond earrings – two earrings, in fact, in each ear. She wore a bright blue and white large-patterned dress with matching scarf thrown over one shoulder. She had a loud, confident voice.

In Betty's car en route to the restaurant, she told me all about bank business and every now and again, she would say to Betty, 'Straight on, dear' or 'Turn left at Broadway, dear' or to Betty about me, 'Isn't she a sweetie?'

When she saw my books that Betty had in the car, she immediately picked up the latest one that I had brought as a gift for Betty and she said, 'I just love this, dear. I'm going to buy it from you.'

Betty said she could have it and Wanda asked me to sign it. Then it occurred to me that the radio people might want to see it because we had a radio interview planned for the very next day. I mentioned this to Betty as we were following Wanda into the restaurant. Once we were settled at our table, Betty asked for the book back temporarily so that the radio people could see it. Wanda gave it back immediately but I detected the hint of displeasure in her eyes and in her bearing. Nevertheless, that evening, Wanda phoned to invite Betty and me to come to dinner with her and her husband on the following Sunday.

I knew by this time that, in most cases, if you're invited for a meal in America, it means that you're going to be taken out to a restaurant rather than having it in the person's home, as would be more the custom here.

The day after we'd had lunch with Wanda and after we'd been to the radio station, Betty took me to see some of the local shops. In a big supermarket, it struck me what a huge and wonderful variety of food there was and I couldn't help remembering the awful shops, most of them half-empty, that I'd seen in the Soviet Union. The shops in America would have been like an absolute wonderland to any Soviet citizen.

Then Betty drove me around to show me some of the houses in the lakeside area. Nearly all of them had an American flag fluttering in front. I couldn't imagine the flying of a Union Jack being a regular feature in the gardens of houses in England, or Scotland (especially Scotland).

On Sunday morning we went to a church and before the service we were invited to sit in on the Sunday School study group. The man taking the Sunday School – who I later discovered was a lawyer – had a mouthful of perfect teeth. I'd never seen such large teeth in my life. He was always showing his teeth, every one of them, top and bottom. He went through the study guide asking us questions and before anyone had the chance to answer, he would give the answer, reading it out of the book with a finger tracing each word. He kept flashing his molars, gritting them and looking at us all straight in the eye and saying, 'Isn't that a wonderful answer, just wonderful!'

The church had a lift and air-conditioning, and a microphone. Betty got up and announced that I was visiting her and I was formally welcomed and given a big round of applause. That evening Wanda and her husband, Earl, arrived in a long-bonneted black car to take us to dinner. Earl looked very handsome with a white beard and white hair. He wore a pale salmon-pink jacket and tie and white shirt and trousers. Wanda wore a shiny patterned trouser suit in different shades of blue and Roman-type sandals.

They took us to a lakeside inn and treated us to a very good meal. After dinner we sat out on the verandah looking out onto the lake. It was dark except for the lakeside lights. It was a warm evening and most of the other male customers wore T-shirts and shorts. There were some real hunks of men with huge brown muscles and chests and they certainly knew how to swagger. I also noticed some enormously fat women in shorts showing their huge buttocks and stomachs.

It was a very enjoyable evening with Wanda doing most of the talking. One of her favourite sayings, I noticed, was, 'If you don't use it, you lose it'. Earl, speaking about the South, said that the rednecks there wore size 18 jackets and size 3 hats and were mostly called Bubba and Dwain.

The next few days were hectic, with different friends and relatives of Betty's taking us around. Each person seemed to think nothing of driving us for hours one way and another and on very hot sunny days. On one occasion, we went to see Lincoln's house and tomb and we waited nearly an hour in a queue out in that roasting sun. I was exhausted and there was Betty standing beside me, at eighty-three years of age and with a stick. She never once complained. I was worried about her and I suggested she sat down on a step.

Eventually Betty's landlord came to collect us in his car and take us to the airport where we were to get a plane to Louisville. I think he must have wanted to prolong his stay in our company because he drove so slowly. He was telling about having been in England during the war and Betty asked him if he would ever go back. He said he thought maybe he'd left it a bit late now. Betty said, 'You must never give up.' and I thought it might be her motto and indicative of her lifestyle.

We were only a short time in Louisville and we had to take a bus in the airport to the other plane we had to catch to Nashville, Tennessee. On the bus, I remember, there was a very handsome young American guy and he looked at Betty and me clutching our hand luggage and bag and he said, 'Y'all all taken off? Run away from home?' Then he turned to me, 'A cheap joke, ma'am, but I couldn't resist it!' He was quite gorgeous and had such a beautiful smile.

When we eventually stepped off the plane in Nashville, the heat hit me as if I'd stepped into an oven. In Nashville we were going to visit a friend of Betty's who lived in a place called Park Minor Presbyterian Apartments. It was a retired people's place and I wondered what it was going to be like. It turned out to be absolutely gorgeous, far nicer than any hotel I'd been in so far. Everything was luxurious. Betty's friend was called Fanny. Her apartment was down a carpeted corridor and it was just like a private flat. She had her own door with her nameplate on it. Inside was the sitting room, with all her own furniture and paintings, and off the room were a fitted kitchen and a beautiful bedroom with a bathroom en suite. A glass door from the sitting room led onto a patio and further on to a lawn and trees. There was a dining room for the residents if they didn't want to cook for themselves.

We went to the dining room and we were a bit late. A plump black waitress said she'd do her best but most things were off the menu. She leaned for a while on the back of one of the chairs and asked me all about myself – where I was from, why I was here, who did I know, and so on. She could hardly believe that this was my first visit to the USA. 'The very first time y'all bin in the good ol' US of A?'

The next day I had an appointment to interview the editor of a newspaper called *The Tennessean*. Regina Lee, the receptionist at the home, fixed Betty and me up with a lift to the newspaper office. By this time I didn't know how I was going to survive the heat but it didn't seem to be bothering anyone else.

The lady who chauffeured us in her car, for instance, was so laid back and southern that it was both screamingly funny and infuriating. She just lay back – literally – with one hand resting loosely on the steering wheel and her other arm stretched across the back of the seat behind Betty. I was sitting in the back seat and this lady kept turning round and asking me questions or making remarks in the laziest, slowest, most southern drawl that I'd so far come across. I was sitting on the edge of my seat with tension because it seemed a miracle to me that we didn't crash into some other car or have some sort of accident.

Soon I was to find out that the journey had been well worth while. It would have been worth any risk. It was the pièce de résistance of my trip so far, indeed of my whole working life up to that point. The editor's name was John Ziegenthaler and what a man! I felt so genuinely honoured to have met him. I was absolutely inspired. It took a special brand of courage for any white person to have marched shoulder to shoulder with the black people, to have spoken out on their behalf and in the name of freedom, to have taken part in all their demonstrations and protests. But for a southern man to have done so took a very special brand of courage indeed.

I decided right there and then to make this man, who had been a hero in real life, the hero in my book *Wounds of War*. I knew of course that I could never do justice to him but at least I would try. I called my fiction character Steve Jackson.

Some time later, I gave another American friend hospitality and when she invited me to visit her home in Long Beach, California, I refused saying that I was busy working on a new book. 'Didn't you tell me that you were doing research on bodyguards for this book?' she asked.

'Yes,' I said.

'Well, if you come over to the States I'll introduce you to the head of security at Paramount Studios in Hollywood. I know him quite well.'

That was of course an offer I couldn't refuse. What a fascinating experience Hollywood turned out to be. I was most interested to explore Sunset Boulevard. The shops and the glamorous shoppers in Rodeo Drive were also worth seeing. I was impressed with the head of Paramount Studios and his large luxurious office, and I wouldn't have missed the tour my friend and I were given of Paramount. But most fascinating of all was my meeting with Thomas G. Hayes, Executive Director of Studio Protection, Operations Division – to give him his full title. Here was another man for whom I was overwhelmed with admiration. What wonderful anecdotes he told me about his experiences with the stars. Apparently he had to keep trying to persuade the bodyguards of the stars not to bring guns on to the set. Elizabeth Taylor's bodyguard was especially protective. As far as I was concerned, Thomas G. Hayes was well worth travelling from Glasgow to listen to.

I have since deeply disagreed with and disliked America's foreign policy and some of their politicians. I can't help remembering, however, the kind and generous-hearted American people that I met on my travels all over the United States.

37

By this time, I was becoming more confident than I had ever thought possible. Apart from travelling to different countries, when I was at home, I was asked more and more to speak at meetings. At one time the mere thought of standing up in front of an audience and speaking in public made me feel quite ill. I'd always to go to a doctor or a chemist beforehand and get something to calm me.

Then I thought of quite a good trick. I decided that once I got up to deliver my talk, I would no longer be Margaret Thomson Davis, I would be an actress acting the part of a confident woman. I got quite practised at this until eventually I was able to stand up and speak quite confidently without thinking myself into the mind of an actress. I didn't need to act a part any more and I began to enjoy public speaking. One of the reasons for that was that I was so often asked to speak in libraries, where most of the audience consisted of my readers who wanted to meet me and tell me how much they'd enjoyed my books. This I've always felt was the reward for all the hard work of writing.

Of course it isn't always plain sailing going around giving talks. I remember one time at the Swanwick Writers' Summer School in England where I was speaking. I had hardly started when a woman at the back suddenly got up and said, 'I'll have to get out of here. I'm falling asleep.' I found out later that she was on medication that made her drowsy but it didn't make me feel any better at the time. It was at that same meeting, after I'd given my talk and there was question time, when a woman said, 'What did you think about Gambia then?'

I'd been talking about technique and structure in short stories so I looked at her and said, 'I don't know what I think about Gambia.'

'You must have thought something about it,' she persisted.

I assured her that I hadn't a thought in my head about Gambia. She was obviously miffed about this and said, 'Well, I expected you to have some thoughts about it after having been there.'

'But I haven't been there,' I said.

'Damn it,' she cried out, 'I've been at the wrong lecture.'

I think it was en route to that particular speaking engagement that I developed a terribly sore back. Friends who were giving me a lift down in their car stopped off some place and they found an osteopath. I explained who I was and where I was going and said that if I didn't get any help with my back, I wouldn't be able to climb up on the platform to give my talk. The osteopath agreed to treat me right there and then without an appointment and he had me on the table, gripped in a half nelson, when he suddenly said, 'I've written a book. Would you read it and tell me what you think of it and what I should do with it?'

I would like to have told him right there and then exactly what to do with it but I was afraid to, in the painful circumstances. So I agreed to take his hundred thousand word manuscript away and read it, then return it with a written critique. It's at this stage, by the way, that one usually discovers the potential writers – the real writers – who one day will be successful, and the others who can't take criticism and haven't the guts or the perseverance to carry on.

I spent a week carefully studying, reading and rereading that man's manuscript and writing a detailed and constructive criticism. He never even said thank you and I never heard from him again. Some people, you see, just want praise, not constructive criticism. I don't know how he would have reacted if he'd received some of the criticism that I've had in my day, not to mention all the rejection slips.

A lot of people fancy being a writer. They have usually a glamorous idea of what that is or imagine it is some sort of soft option, mostly because the writer usually works at home. Some people think that because you're at home, you're not working, or at least you can knock off at any time or for any length of time at the drop of a hat. Don't you believe it! In fact, it's quite the reverse. It wouldn't be too much of an exaggeration to say that a writer's work is never done.

People have said to me, 'Why don't you just switch off when you leave your desk?' But if you're in the middle of writing a book, you can't do that – at least, I certainly can't. My characters are alive in my mind. I can still see them in my mind's eye moving about, I can still hear them talking, I still feel for them and with them.

I often come across people who don't feel that writing is hard work and others who think you must make a fortune. Many a time when I've been in a taxi, the driver has said to me, 'Is this you just getting home from your work?' and I say, 'Well no, actually I work at home.'

'Oh, what do you do?' he'll ask.

'I'm a writer – I write books.'

The reply to that is invariably, 'Oh, by Jove, you're lucky! You must be rolling in it!'

They never believe me when I tell them that I haven't made a fortune. I do feel lucky, though, being able to go around and meet so many of my readers. I also feel I'm fortunate in belonging to Glasgow because I meet so many potential characters for my novels. So often I get dialogue more or less handed to me on a plate – especially humorous dialogue. At one of the launches that there used to be on the Clyde – important affairs they were and there were always some of the directors on the platform with their wives or at least a couple of VIP ladies – just before one of the ladies was about to perform the ceremony, there was a downpour of rain and the managing director called down to the crowd of workmen, 'Is there a big macintosh to cover these two ladies?' One of the workmen shouted back, 'No, but there's a wee McGregor willing to try his best!' I could never just imagine dialogue like that.

I remember a friend telling me about a very dignified academic dinner he attended in Glasgow. All the academics were in their hooded gowns. A wee waitress was bustling round the back of everybody serving the vegetables when she suddenly shouted, 'Oh ah'm awfae sorry, son, ah've drapped some peas doon yer pixie.'

Another time this friend told me about an important dinner where the guests were all foreign dignitaries. Most of the dishes on the menu were foreign as well. But there was spinach on the menu and one person had ordered it. Eventually the waitress arrived with the spinach and called out, 'Who's Popeye?'

Yet another waitress anecdote concerned a friend's small hotel. She'd forgotten to put fish on the menu and as it was a Friday and she thought there might be Catholics among the guests, she instructed the waitress to discreetly find out how many people wanted fish so that they knew how much to prepare in the kitchen. Then to her horror she heard the waitress shout out in the dining room, 'Hands up yous yins that are the Catholics!'

When I have a Glasgow waitress as a character in one of my books, I will make an amalgam of these three waitresses and oh, how I will love the character and how I will enjoy writing about her.

38

Not only dialogue is handed to me on a plate. At times, whole stories are pressed upon me. Once a woman came up to me and said, 'What are you writing at the moment, Margaret?'

I'd never seen the woman before but everybody knows me as Margaret and I said, 'Well, to tell you the truth, the only thing I have in my mind at the moment is religious bigotry.'

She cried out, 'Oh, you should meet my mother!'

'Really?' I said. 'Is your mother a religious bigot?'

'Oh yes,' she assured me, and she began to tell me that she had been very much in love with this boy when she was just a girl and he was in love with her. When her mother found out that he was of a different religion, she forbade her to have anything more to do with the boy, even to talk to him. Not long after that, her mother made her marry another, older, man, who was a member of her church. They were all very religious. I don't know if it was some kind of sect that that family belonged to, including the girl. I called her Andrina in the book. Apparently she sang like an angel in the choir.

She went on to tell me that a year or two after she was married, and she'd had a child by this time, she met her first boyfriend again. She just bumped into him one day and he told her that he'd been following her and watching her and could even tell her what she'd been wearing on different occasions.

It occurred to me that here was a theme of obsession and an interesting story. She went on to say that they began a secret love affair. Now I didn't think this woman would speak to me on to my tape-recorder about such an intimate subject.

However, you never get anywhere unless you try, so I said to her, 'Would you come to my house one day and tell me all about this secret love affair on to my tape-recorder and give me permission to use it in a book?'

I explained of course that it would be used within the framework of fiction – nobody would be able to recognise her. To my surprise she said yes. In fact she was delighted and she came to my house on several occasions. I have piles of tapes all with her spilling the beans. I'd never heard the like of it in my life. I discovered 'in fact' that I had never lived!

At one stage she even brought her lover to my house so that he could tell me his side of it. The poor man was embarrassed but the woman, apparently oblivious of his sensitivities, kept prompting him and when she wasn't doing that, she was chatting happily about herself. When I told my son about the lovers' visit, he said, 'For goodness' sake, Mum, they'll be giving you a bloomin' demonstration next!'

Of course, I would draw the line at that. After all, imagination has to come in to it somewhere. But, you know, it wasn't really the passionate and very sexy affair that triggered me to write the book, that gave me the motivation to launch into all the hard work – it was the religious hypocrisy.

All during this time of secret and sexual high jinks, this woman was still attending church and singing in the choir. In between church attendances, choir practices, and so on, she was telling all sorts of lies to her husband and her mother in order to get away to be with her lover. She told me that one night it had been so beautiful, it had been a religious experience. She said that, if they'd had time in the morning, they would have gone to church but instead they lay in bed in each other's arms and listened to Gregorian chants on his tape machine.

I wouldn't have felt either surprised or shocked if she'd just said that she'd enjoyed a good night's bonking. But to talk about a religious experience was too much.

In this context, after all the lies she'd told and the web of deceit she'd woven round her life, I couldn't help thinking, 'Oh dear, oh dear, oh dear!'

For hours, days, weeks, I listened to this woman. She was obviously an extroverted kind of person who enjoyed talking about herself and her experiences. She was also very beautiful and despite what I thought about religious hypocrisy, I couldn't help liking her. In many ways she was a very likeable person and had great warmth and charm.

What human being can really know what is inside another person's mind or heart? Even a writer can't do that with total certainty.

He can do that with his fictional characters. He does know what's in their hearts and minds. I had to go into the mind of this main character that I called Andrina in my book.

I feel that a reader needs to have some sort of sympathy or at least understanding of a main character in a book, if only to give them some measure of identification with that character. I suspected that readers would have some difficulty with sympathetic understanding of Andrina.

To make her more understandable and to engender some sympathy for her, I made her have an unhappy childhood in the book. Now this woman had told me she had a perfectly happy childhood. Indeed it sounded as if she'd been rather spoiled. From then on, her life always seemed to work out exactly as she wanted it to. My idea of the unhappy childhood creating sympathy and compassion for the character didn't quite seem to work out. I'm not sure what readers felt but I do know that when I was interviewed by male journalists and radio people, they all began by saying the same thing.

'Oh, I enjoyed your new book, Margaret, but what a bitch!'

I became very worried about this because by this time I'd given the woman a free copy of the first book and I was afraid that she would be upset if this was indeed the impression that

I'd given of the character. All I knew was that I'd recorded as truthfully as I could exactly what she had told me about the details of her affair.

It was set in a framework of fiction, of course. The characters had different jobs from the real people. They lived in different places and apart from the sexual affair, different things happened to them.

It turned out I had no need to worry.

My book apparently confirmed her romantic view of herself and she was absolutely delighted with it.

39

The first book of that trilogy was called *Hold Me Forever*. The second one was called *Kiss Me No More* and the third *A Kind of Immortality*. I have never liked the first two titles. They were given to me by a writer friend because I couldn't think of any myself – or at least I did think of one for the first book but the publisher wouldn't have it.

The woman had told me at one point that her lover had said to her after making love on one occasion that she was so soft and feminine, yet so passionate, she held him like a velvet vice. I thought, 'Oh, a velvet vice, that sounds a good title', and so I put that on my manuscript and sent it to off.

The publisher phoned me up and said, 'Oh, we can't have that, Margaret! It sounds pornographic.'

Titles are very difficult to think of and as I couldn't come up with another at that point, this writer friend supplied me with *Hold Me Forever*. I couldn't think of a suitable one for the second book either and a poet friend suggested *Kiss Me No More*. The publisher loved both those titles but I felt they made the books sound too romantic and in actual fact, as in most of my other books, there was a gritty realism.

When I came to write the second book, and the third one, although Andrina's story runs through each, in the second and third books, Andrina steps a little into the background and a fresh main character takes over in the second one, and yet another fresh main character takes centre stage in the third.

I decided to make the lover character a man who started work as a bouncer in pubs and clubs and then, because he was an intelligent and ambitious man, he works his way up to employing a great many other bouncers, and then starts a security business, and then gets into bodyguarding and all sorts of related areas.

As part of that research, I picked out the biggest security business I could find in the Yellow Pages and wrote to the address there, said who I was and gave a brief biography and a selection of reviews of my books. I explained that I was in the middle of researching this book and I wanted to create a character as I've just described.

I got a letter back from the man who owned this security business saying he was on his way to a world tour with Paul McCartney but when he came back, he would be very pleased to come and help me all he could because my letter had intrigued him. The fact was that the letter had described his career in exact detail. The man came to my house eventually – indeed he visited me several times – and I have him on tape telling me the most fascinating stories about some of his work experiences, especially as a bodyguard.

I admired him enormously. He was absolutely gorgeous but not a bit conceited or big-headed – either about himself or his job. For the first time in my life, I wished I was thirty years younger. Not that that would have made any difference because as well as being a comparatively young man, he was happily married.

My feelings about him gave me the theme of the third book of that trilogy. With the usual technique I use in creating stories and characters in my novels, I took one aspect or feeling or characteristic and I exaggerated it and also gave my imagination free flow.

So one of the storylines in the third book was the love of an older woman for a younger man. I mentioned this to my son. He always reads my manuscripts now and he is a good critic and help to me. He thought this story line was a very good idea but he said, 'Make the man in his twenties, Mum, and the woman perhaps forty, because nobody could fancy a woman of your age.'

Anyway, I didn't worry because I thoroughly enjoyed writing the book and the passionate love affair between the forty-year-old Bessie and the twenty-something Sean. By the way, both Bernard and Sean in the book were modelled from the same man in real life and I'll always remember him with admiration and affection.

Andrina's lover, in *Hold Me Forever*, is Bernard. In the book he is a member of a big family. I decided to set this family in a place called Blackhill, simply because I'd never written about that area before. The book was set in the sixties, and in the sixties Blackhill was real gangster land. The man known as the Glasgow Godfather lived there.

Normally when I research where my characters will live, I walk about the area until I get to know it very well. I hesitated a wee bit about wandering about on my own in Blackhill. I had also to find jobs for all my characters. I was beginning to run out of jobs, especially for this lover's brothers. Eventually I settled on one of the characters being a boxer. I knew nothing about boxing and so that was another worry. How was I going to find out about that?

The third difficult research aspect about that book was the addiction theme that I decided on – in other words there was to be an alcoholic in the book.

So these were three difficult areas I had to find out about, no doubt spend a great deal of time finding out about: Blackhill, alcoholism and boxing. I decided, however, that before I started work on these three subjects, I must fulfil a reading engagement I'd promised to do in the back room of Sammy Dow's pub in Nithsdale Road. So I went along to this pub on the evening of the reading engagement. The reading I gave was from another of my books, *A Sense of Belonging*. It was a chapter set in old Garngad which was quite a tough area as well.

After I'd read the chapter, a man came up to me and said, 'Here, Margaret, I enjoyed that, partly because I was born in Garngad. I was brought up in Blackhill but . . .'

'Hold it right there,' I cried out. 'Would you come to my house tomorrow and tell me on to my tape-recorder all about your memories of being brought up in Blackhill?'

He agreed and my friends and my son as well – not for the first time – said I was crazy. I meet a perfect stranger in a pub, a stranger who's been brought up in Blackhill of all places, and I ask him to my home.

In my excitement at finding someone to help me, I'd never thought of any risk angle. Hughie, although a real tough guy, was at the same time a decent and good-hearted man. But that first afternoon when he visited me, I knew nothing about him. When he came in he said, 'Right, Margaret, what do ye want, hen?'

And I launched eagerly into my research requirements about Blackhill. He immediately came up trumps with the most marvellous human details about day-to-day living there – things that I could never have found in books. Really marvellous material! Halfway through the afternoon though, I remembered my duties as a hostess and said, 'Oh here, Hughie, would you like a wee drink because I've got a nice malt whisky there?'

'No thanks, hen,' he said. 'I'm an alcoholic.'

'Wonderful!' I cried. Here was something else he could help me with. It turned out he'd not had a drink for twenty years and now he did work for AA, who had helped him in the first place.

I said to him, 'Oh, I'm so glad you're cured, Hughie.'

He said, 'Margaret, did you not hear what I said? I'm an alcoholic. I'm always just one drink away from the gutter.' For the rest of the afternoon, he gave me such a wonderful insight into the mind of an alcoholic. At the end of the afternoon I said to him, 'Hughie, thank you so much. You've been such a wonderful help to me. You've saved me weeks, maybe months of work. Now all I've got to worry about is finding out about boxing.'

'I used to be a boxer,' Hughie said. What a bit of luck! He then told me all about his local boxing clubs and the boxers training in the ring and the gangsters gambling around it and the walls and the ceiling brown with years of tobacco smoke. Real atmospheric stuff I could never have imagined. Hughie came to the party for the launch of that book and his ex-wife came along with him. In the printed acknowledgements at the front of the book, I had included Hughie's name and I'd said that he was a wee gem. His ex-wife came up to me when I was signing copies and she said, 'You wouldn't have called him a wee gem if you'd known him when I knew him.'

I read a chapter from the book which featured Scobie, who was the alcoholic character in the book, and afterwards Hughie came up to me and he said, 'You know, Margaret, I was never nearer to tears because you made that character so realistic and it reminded me of some of the worst years in my life.'

A character in the second book, *Kiss Me No More*, was a secondary school teacher. I'd already had a primary teacher in another book, *A Sense of Belonging*, but this was a secondary teacher so I spoke to a great many teachers and visited various schools – did quite a bit of in-depth research, in fact. I had always appreciated that teaching was a difficult, demanding and often very stressful job, but it wasn't until I did this research that I realised just how stressful it could be, especially in some of the tougher areas of Glasgow.

I remember one man – a retired teacher who'd had to take early retirement because of stress – told me many stories and anecdotes but one in particular sticks in my mind. He arrived at school one morning and as soon as he got to his classroom door, he knew there was something wrong because there was silence. Normally the first thing he had to do each morning was quell a riot. But everything was silent.

He went into his classroom and the first thing that caught his eye was this boy sitting in the front row holding a gun and aiming it at him. This boy's father was a well-known gangster, and Murdo, the teacher, knew right away that the gun must belong to the boy's father. He was feverishly trying to think of the best way to cope with this situation. He didn't want to go out of the classroom again in case this boy took it into his head to spray the other pupils with bullets. So he walked up to a cupboard at the back of the class to get something out of it, and all the time the boy kept pointing the gun at him. Murdo came back and sat down at his desk and the boy still kept the gun on him.

Murdo, remembering how fascinated this boy was with guns – and how knowledgeable he was – engaged him in conversation. He said, 'What kind of gun is that?' The boy's face lit up with interest and he told Murdo exactly what kind of gun it was and all about it. They chatted away for a while like this and then Murdo asked to have a look at it. The boy handed it up in the proper way, holding the muzzle, and Murdo examined it, although he didn't know a thing about guns.

Then he said to the boy, 'Look, son, do you not think it would be a good idea if I kept this gun in my desk until you're ready to go home and then you can take it back to your father?'

The boy said, 'Aye, OK.' and that was that. But Murdo said to me, 'You know, Margaret, I had a full day's teaching to do after that and my legs were like jelly. And by the way,' he added, 'that boy, later in life, spent a long time in jail for gun running and eventually died by the gun.'

I heard some humorous stories too, but those mostly came from primary school teachers. I remember one telling me that she was teaching in what we used to call the baby class – the first class – and this wee chap on his first day at school asked to go to the toilet. The teacher pointed him in the right direction and off he went. He was away for an awfully long time and she began to get worried. All at once the door opened and he appeared in the doorway with his trousers round his ankles and asked, 'Who wipes the bums in this place?'

Nowadays though, even in primary schools, teachers suffer some terrible stress as well as verbal and even physical abuse. By the time I came to the third book in that trilogy, I felt that because I had dealt with religious bigotry in the first two, I really ought to be fair-handed and portray a good Christian woman in the third book. I decided to make her a Quaker, not because I believe Quakers are any better than anyone else, simply because I knew something about Quaker beliefs and forms of worship and I thought it would save me a lot of work. I wouldn't need to do nearly so much research.

So I started the book and it was soon to prove very difficult. I'd forgotten how difficult it was to write about a good person without being boring. It's lovely to meet good people in real life but to write about them in a novel is quite a different matter. A story has to have first of all a problem for the main characters. It's got to have tensions, conflicts and a suspense quality that keeps the reader turning the page to see what's going to happen next.

The main character in it was a painter, an artist – although for much of the time an unrecognised and unappreciated one. As usual I gave the manuscript to my son to read. Normally my son and daughter-in-law and my grandsons came for lunch on a Sunday but this time Kenneth phoned me in the middle of the week and said, 'Look, Mum, do you mind if I come on my own on Sunday? I want to talk to you about this book.'

I thought, 'Oh, oh.' I knew – and had known from the beginning – that all was not well with it. Anyway, he came along on the Sunday and we started to discuss it. It was as I feared.

He said, 'You know, Mum, this character of Bessie is totally unbelievable. She's too good to be true. She has apparently no faults or weaknesses. It doesn't matter what awful thing anyone says or does to her, she just absorbs it all with no emotional reaction. No anger. No resentment. Nothing.'

I said, 'You're quite right, son. I'll have to start it again.' And I did start writing the book again. This time I gave Bessie plenty of faults and frailties. Mind you, she's still a good woman in the end, in a practical sense, but I start the book with a scene in Quaker meeting for worship. All the Quakers are sitting, heads bowed in silent prayer. Bessie, however, is thinking randy thoughts about some man she fancies. Poor old Bessie has plenty of problems in her life after that but she's now human and believable and she struggles throughout the book to cope with them as best she can.

I've struggled to continue writing books as best I can. I say 'struggle' because there's no denying that writing is hard work. But I enjoy doing it. I have written well over twenty novels now, and although my spirit (and my imagination) is still as strong and willing as ever, physically I'm not as strong as I was. For instance, after the Clydesiders trilogy, I was really exhausted. In that trilogy, I was a soldier struggling on the beaches of Dunkirk. I was a pilot in a Spitfire in the Battle of Britain. And I was suffering the horrors of both the London and the Clydebank blitz.

I was not just exhausted as a result, I was a nervous wreck. Of course, to some degree or other, I always feel shattered when I finish writing a book. I've to go to my doctor every time I finish work. There I always get a row and am told to remember that I'm not a young woman any more. I've *got* to pace myself and get more rest. I always promise that I'll definitely do that next time.

One book was called *A Darkening of the Heart* and one of the main characters is the poet, Robert Burns. I'm a fan of

Burns and it was a book I'd always wanted to write. I decided that the first thing I'd do for research was to follow Burns' footsteps wherever he went. To my surprise, and some chagrin, I discovered there was hardly a spot in Scotland he hadn't visited. So there I was stravaiging all over the place, getting exhausted before I'd hardly started any work on the book.

It had to be a novel, of course, because I'm a novelist. So I added a fictitious family – an elderly doctor and his wife, their young doctor son called Alexander and their daughter Susanna. That meant I had to do research on medicine in the eighteenth century and that really upset me. Especially when I read about what poor Robert Burns had to suffer at the hands of doctors. They actually killed him. Not intentionally, of course. They were only acting within the knowledge – or, rather, lack of knowledge – of the time. In the course of my in-depth research I uncovered many myths and stories that people have always believed about Burns that are untrue and have harmed his reputation.

He knew this would happen, of course. On his deathbed he told a friend that there would be poems published that were unfinished and that he wouldn't wish to be published. There would be others published in his name that he had never written at all. There would be scandalous and untrue things said about him after he was gone and unable to defend himself against them. And all these things have come to pass.

One reviewer said of the book:

> The author has skilfully interwoven known historical events in the poet's life with the fictional world of Alexander and Susanna. This novel could easily have become nothing more than a catalogue of Burns' achievements but in the hands of a master storyteller it is, instead, a page-turning saga.

Another reviewer praised the book highly and I was particularly pleased at one sentence in the review, 'She obviously knows her Burns.'

My agent, when she first read the manuscript, phoned me from England and said that she'd never thought much about Burns before but 'you've actually brought him to life as a man'.

I liked that because he'd come so alive to me as a man.

The Mitchell Library thought highly of the book too, and as well as giving it pride of place on their shelves in their Burns Room, they gave me a wonderful launch party there as well.

I'd hardly finished that book when I began getting an idea for yet another. This one was different again. Readers often tell me three things they like about my books. First of all, my books always have good strong stories. Secondly, they always learn something from them, whether it's medicine in the eighteenth century or as in my later book, *A Deadly Deception*, about women's refuges and life in a high-rise flat and the interweaving stories of some of the other tenants in the building. Thirdly, readers tell me that all my books are fresh and different. I don't just repeat the same story over and over again, they say, as some writers do.

Well, *A Deadly Deception* is certainly different again. It's a crime thriller and it's the first time I've attempted one of those. But the characters and the story came to life for me, just as they always do as I'm writing. In this story, there is one very scary scene in a bakery and café in Bearsden. Recently I was meeting someone in Bearsden. I arrived too early so I thought I'd go into this café for a cup of tea to pass the time before going to the arranged meeting place. Believe it or not, I could not bring myself to set foot in the café. I just didn't have the nerve. I knew I was being ridiculous. I knew perfectly well that I'd made the whole scary scene up. The whole story along with everyone in it was only a figment of my imagination. But, you see, I found out long ago that, if the story feels real to the writer, it'll feel real to the reader. And that's a good thing. It's part of the job and I've just got to live with it.

This time the agent didn't phone me. She sent a letter saying that congratulations were due for *A Deadly Deception*. She said it was very different from anything I'd ever done before and it was the best thing I'd ever done – 'A real gritty, gripping read from page one to the end.'

One reviewer said it was television almost as it stood. My literary agent agreed and passed it on to a television agent. Also, my publisher told me that a BBC radio producer had e-mailed him asking for a copy of the book to be sent to him. As a result, I'm hoping that this book will be a big best-seller and make my fortune. Not that I'm bothered for myself. At my age now, and with my rather painful osteoporosis, I don't feel like travelling abroad any more, for instance. As a Quaker, I'm supposed to live simply and so I neither need nor want any luxuries. All I want is the security of having enough money to pay my rent and electricity, heating, phone and food bills.

But oh, I would love to be able to help my family by clearing their mortgages and by helping with the education of my grandchildren.

Of course, I always live in hope that each book I write will prove to be a big best-seller. I dream of television drama-tisations and films being made of my work.

And I'm not going to give up hope. No, never. But I must confess that I'm getting more and more exhausted after each book. As I think I mentioned before, my spirit and my imagination are as strong as ever. It's just the old flesh that keeps getting weaker.

A Deadly Deception had the theme of fear and, in my usual fashion, I worked myself into the story and characters to such a degree that I felt particularly shattered and exhausted by the time I'd finished because of the emotional nature of the theme.

The fear engendered by the book still clung to me. More

that that, it struck a chord and reawakened all the fears of my childhood. I could not shake them off. Instead, I was sucked back by dark terrors far more frightening than I could imagine in any book.

Their shadows returned to haunt me. I felt the same anguish in old age as I felt as a young child. It is only the outward shell that is old. Inside, oh inside, I'm still that frightened, bewildered, helpless little girl. I cringed in some darkened room, I don't know where. I feared a strange man approaching me. I cowered in a corner of a shadowy hole-in-the-wall bed, eyes enormous, fists tightly clutching the sheets up against my mouth in a futile effort to protect myself. So many other places. So many other terrors.

Yet, during my lifetime, so many good things have also happened to me. A few years ago, for instance, I experienced one of the happiest days of my life when, in the magnificent banqueting hall of the Glasgow City Chambers, I was presented on behalf of the citizens of Glasgow with the Lord Provost's Award for Literature and for 'bringing Glasgow's history to vibrant life'.

And I have a wonderful, loving family. I also have many kind and loving friends and I'm so grateful to them all.

Yet, deep down, there is still that child, alone and in anguish.

I found an anonymous poem recently that, to use a Quaker phrase, 'speaks to my condition'.

I suddenly am plagued at night with fears
not recognised at first,
as those of that forgotten child within,
her presence silenced by necessity
to let her go from my maturing
noisy years.

She returns unbidden now,
and weeping on my barrier

leans with all her rending terrors.
Longings too, that choke the throat
come sweeping through with cries and pains
I cannot silence,
nor contain in sleep.

Dear child, come hold my hand, that is your hand too,
and I will love you with another love you did not have–
into another of love's dimensions, O so close,
child hold me tight, for I have need of you,
and we will walk together–
through dark, through light.

How will I ever be able to bear the thought of writing another book? Rest, the doctor said. How can I rest when I am so desperately unhappy and tormented?

I leave my desk to go out for a walk. Soon I find myself, despite my state of mind, gazing up at the beautiful architecture of Glasgow with flickers of admiration. Gradually some of my loneliness begins to evaporate. More and more the warm, friendly bustle of the Glasgow people and the noisy symphony of the street entertainers enfold me.

But wait, now what is happening? I'm actually experiencing tremors of excitement. Something has given me a great idea for another book. Energy is beginning to surge through me. Then suddenly I know what Steinbeck meant when he said, 'I am pleased with myself for no reason at all. I have a good golden light in my stomach which is a mesh of happiness.'

And, as Stephen King said in his marvellous autobiography, *On Writing*:

Writing isn't about making money, getting famous, getting dates, getting laid, or making friends. In the end, it's about enriching the lives of those who will read your work, and enriching your own life as well. It's about getting up, getting well and getting over. Getting happy, okay? Getting happy.

Some of this book – perhaps too much – has been about how I learned to do it. Much of it has been how you can do it better. The rest of it – and perhaps the best of it – is a permission slip: you can, you should and, if you're brave enough to start, *you will.*

Writing is magic, as much the water of life as any other creative art. The water is free. So drink.

Drink and be filled up.